The Sacred Art of Silence - How Silence Speaks in Scripture

Joshua Rhoades

Published by Joshua Paul Rhoades, 2024.

While every precaution has been taken in the preparation of this book, the publisher assumes no responsibility for errors or omissions, or for damages resulting from the use of the information contained herein.

THE SACRED ART OF SILENCE - HOW SILENCE SPEAKS IN SCRIPTURE

First edition. August 22, 2024.

ISBN: 979-8227533890

Written by Joshua Rhoades.

Also by Joshua Rhoades

Courage Under Fire: David's Stand On The Battlefield
Jonah's Journey: Voices Of Redemption And Lessons In Obedience
The Furnace Of Faith: 12 Principles From The Heat Of Faith
Whispers of Hope: Inspiring Stories of Men's Prayers In Scripture
Frontier Legends: The Oregon Dream
Elijah: A Beacon Of Boldness
HOOK, LINE & SAVIOUR - Faith Reflections from Fishing
Driven By Faith: Motor Racing Inspired Christian Life
30 Day Devotional - Bold and Strong- Coffee Devotions for a
Courageous Christian Walk
Authentic Christianity: The Heart of Old Time Religion
Flee Fornication: The Plea For Purity
Renewed Hope- How to Find Encouragement in God
Sounding The Call - The Voice of Conviction
The Altar - Where Heaven Meets Earth
The Sacred Art of Silence - How Silence Speaks in Scripture

Table of Contents

Introduction

In a world dominated by noise, endless chatter, and constant distractions, the power of silence has become a forgotten art. We live in an era where words are abundant, yet meaning is often lost. We fill our days with sounds—voices, music, the hum of technology—believing that in the rush of activity, we are making progress, moving forward. But what if the true path to wisdom, peace, and spiritual growth lies not in the clamor, but in the quiet spaces in between? What if silence is not an absence, but a presence—an invitation to connect with something deeper, more profound? "The Sacred Art of Silence - How Silence Speaks in Scripture" invites you on a journey to rediscover the transformative power of silence as taught through the pages of the Bible.

Throughout Scripture, silence is not merely the absence of sound; it is a dynamic force, a tool used by God to teach, guide, and transform His people. From the stillness that preceded creation to the quiet moments of reflection in the lives of prophets and saints, the Bible is rich with examples of how silence can speak louder than words. This book delves into these sacred moments, exploring how silence is woven into the fabric of Scripture and how it can be woven into the fabric of our lives.

In these pages, you will encounter stories of individuals who found strength, wisdom, and clarity in moments of silence. You will learn how silence can be a response to God's call, a demonstration of trust, and a pathway to deeper understanding. The Bible shows us that silence is not passive; it is an active choice to step back, to listen, and to wait on God. As one meditates upon the Words of Scripture, it is in these moments of quiet that we can hear God's voice most clearly, that we can understand His will, and that we can grow in our relationship with Him.

This book is not just an exploration of biblical silence; it is a guide to cultivating the art of silence in your own life. Each chapter will lead you through the ways in which silence can enrich your spiritual journey—how it can help you develop wisdom and understanding, guard your soul, demonstrate patience, and deepen your prayer life. You will discover how silence can cultivate peace and foster spiritual growth. Most importantly, you will see how silence is a powerful expression of trust in God, allowing Him to fight your battles and guide your path.

As you read, you will be encouraged to practice silence in your daily life, to create moments of stillness where you can spend time with the Lord and reflect on His Word. In a world that values noise and activity, embracing silence can be countercultural, but it is in this sacred quiet that true transformation happens. "The Sacred Art of Silence - How Silence Speaks in Scripture" is more than a book; it is an invitation to step into the silence, to listen for God's voice through the reading and meditation of His Word, and to experience the profound peace and strength that comes from resting in His presence.

Let these pages inspire you to reclaim the power of silence, to find the sacred in the stillness, and to allow God's voice to speak louder than the noise of the world.

Chapter 1 - Digging into Wisdom and Understanding

Silence is a powerful and important concept in the Bible, particularly in the King James Version (KJV). It is often associated with wisdom, understanding, and spiritual growth. In Proverbs 17:28, the Bible tells us, "Even a fool, when he holdeth his peace, is counted wise: and he that shutteth his lips is esteemed a man of understanding." This verse shows us that silence can be a sign of wisdom and understanding. Even if someone does not have much wisdom, they can still appear wise by knowing when to keep quiet instead of speaking carelessly. Silence can prevent us from saying things that might cause harm or make us look foolish. By choosing to remain silent, we show that we understand the importance of thoughtful speech and the value of listening. In Proverbs 21:23, we read, "Whoso keepeth his mouth and his tongue keepeth his soul from troubles." This verse reminds us that silence can protect us from trouble. When we control our words and refrain from speaking hastily, we avoid unnecessary conflicts and problems. The Bible teaches us that silence is not only about avoiding trouble, but it is also about demonstrating patience and wisdom. In Ecclesiastes 3:7, we learn that there is "a time to keep silence, and a time to speak." This verse helps us understand that there are moments in life when silence is the best response, and knowing when to be silent is a sign of true wisdom. Silence also allows us to reflect and grow spiritually. In Lamentations 3:26, it says, "It is good that a man should both hope and quietly wait for the salvation of the Lord." This verse shows that silence is a way to patiently wait on the Lord, trusting in His timing and plan. Through silence, we can connect more deeply with God and find peace in His presence. The Bible also warns us about the dangers of talking too much. Proverbs 10:19 teaches, "In the multitude of words there wanteth not sin: but he that refraineth his lips is wise." This verse suggests that when we talk too much, we are more likely to say things that are wrong or hurtful. By practicing silence, we show wisdom and avoid the pitfalls of careless speech. Silence is also linked to peace. In James 1:19, we are advised, "Let every man be swift to hear, slow to speak, slow to wrath." This verse connects silence with listening and patience, showing that when we are slow to speak and quick to listen, we are less likely to become angry and more likely to promote peace in our relationships. Silence is also a way to deepen our prayer life. In Psalm 46:10, God tells us, "Be still, and know that I am God." This verse invites us to find stillness and silence in our lives, where we can focus on God and recognize His power and presence. Silence, in this context, is not just about being quiet but about creating space to experience God's presence more fully. Silence can also be a sign of humility and reverence before God. In Habakkuk 2:20, it says, "But the Lord is in his holy temple: let all the earth keep silence before him." This verse encourages us to approach God with a quiet and humble heart, acknowledging His greatness and our own smallness. By being silent before God, we show our respect and awe for His majesty. Silence can also help us avoid conflict. Proverbs 15:1 teaches, "A soft answer turneth away wrath: but grievous words stir up anger." Sometimes, choosing to remain silent or to respond gently can calm a situation and prevent it from escalating into a conflict. On the other hand, harsh or thoughtless words can make things worse. Silence encourages us to think carefully before we speak. In Proverbs 13:3, it says, "He that keepeth his mouth keepeth his life: but he that openeth wide his lips shall have destruction." This verse highlights the importance of controlling our speech. Silence can protect us from making rash decisions or saying things that could lead to harm or regret. Silence is also a way to promote spiritual growth. In Isaiah 30:15, we read, "For thus saith the Lord God, the Holy One of Israel; In returning and rest shall ye be saved; in quietness and in confidence shall be your strength." This verse shows that silence, or quietness, is linked to strength and confidence in the Lord. By embracing silence, we can grow stronger in our faith and our reliance on God. Silence can also be a demonstration of trust in God. In Exodus 14:14, we are reassured, "The Lord shall fight for you, and ye shall hold your peace." This verse shows that sometimes the best thing we can do is to remain silent and trust that God will handle the situation. By holding our peace, we show our faith in God's ability to protect and provide for us. Throughout the Bible, silence is portrayed as a sacred and powerful practice. It is a way to demonstrate wisdom, understanding, patience, and trust in God. Silence helps us avoid unnecessary trouble, promotes peace in our relationships, and allows us to grow spiritually. By practicing silence, we create space to listen to God's voice, reflect on His word, and experience His presence more deeply. Silence is not just the absence of speech; it is an active and intentional choice to be still and to focus on what truly matters. In a world that is often noisy and chaotic, the Bible reminds us of the importance of finding moments of silence where we can connect with God, reflect on our lives, and find peace in His presence. The sacred art of silence is a timeless and valuable practice that can lead to greater wisdom, understanding, and spiritual growth. The Bible, especially in the King James Version, teaches us that silence speaks volumes, and sometimes the most powerful thing we can do is to say nothing at all.

Chapter 2 - Defending One's Soul

Silence is a powerful tool in life, and the Bible, particularly in the King James Version (KJV), speaks about it in many ways, highlighting how silence can protect us and keep us from unnecessary trouble. One of the key verses that teach us about the importance of silence is Proverbs 21:23, which says, "Whoso keepeth his mouth and his tongue keepeth his soul from troubles." This verse reminds us that by being careful with our words and practicing silence, we can avoid many problems that could arise from speaking too quickly or saying things without thinking. The Bible often connects our speech with our well-being, showing that what we say can have a big impact on our lives. When we speak without thinking, we can create conflicts, misunderstandings, and hurt feelings. But when we practice silence and control our words, we are better able to maintain peace and avoid these kinds of troubles. Silence is not just about not talking; it is about being thoughtful and intentional with our words. It's about knowing when it's better to listen than to speak, and when it's better to hold back our words to avoid causing harm. The Bible teaches that silence can be a way of guarding our souls, protecting ourselves from the consequences of careless speech. In many situations, saying too much or saying the wrong thing can lead to arguments, damaged relationships, and even more serious consequences. By keeping silent, we give ourselves time to think, to consider the impact of our words, and to choose whether or not speaking is the best course of action. In the KJV, there are other verses that support this idea of silence as a way of guarding our soul. For example, in Proverbs 10:19, it says, "In the multitude of words there wanteth not sin: but he that refraineth his lips is wise." This verse tells us that when we talk a lot, there is more opportunity for sin to occur, but if we hold back our words, we show wisdom. Wisdom in the Bible is often linked with knowing when to speak and when to remain silent. It's about understanding the power of words and using them carefully and thoughtfully. Another verse that highlights the importance of silence is Proverbs 13:3, which says, "He that keepeth his mouth keepeth his life: but he that openeth wide his lips shall have destruction." This verse directly connects the control of our speech with the preservation of our life. It suggests that those who are careful with their words are more likely to avoid destruction, while those who speak without thinking are more likely to bring trouble upon themselves. Silence, therefore, is not just a passive state of not talking; it is an active practice of guarding our soul, protecting our well-being, and making wise choices about when and how we speak. The Bible also teaches us that silence can be a way of avoiding unnecessary conflict. In Proverbs 15:1, it says, "A soft answer turneth away wrath: but grievous words stir up anger." This verse shows us that how we respond to others can either calm a situation or make it worse. Sometimes, the best way to turn away wrath or avoid anger is to remain silent or to respond in a gentle, controlled manner. Silence can prevent us from saying things in the heat of the moment that we might later regret. It gives us time to cool down, to think about the situation, and to respond in a way that is more likely to lead to peace rather than conflict. The Bible's teachings on silence are not just about avoiding trouble or conflict; they are also about the deeper spiritual practice of self-control. In James 1:19, we are instructed, "Wherefore, my beloved brethren, let every man be swift to hear, slow to speak, slow to wrath." This verse encourages us to listen more and speak less, to be slow to anger and quick to understand. Silence is a way of practicing self-control, of taking the time to listen and understand before we speak. It's about being patient, thoughtful, and intentional in our communication. In a world where there is often so much noise, where people are quick to speak and slow to listen, the Bible's teachings on silence offer a different way of living. They encourage us to slow down, to be more mindful of our words, and to recognize the power of silence in guarding our soul and maintaining peace in our lives. Silence is also a way of demonstrating humility and respect. In Proverbs 11:12, it says, "He that is void of wisdom despiseth his neighbour: but a man of understanding holdeth his peace." This verse suggests that holding our peace, or remaining silent, can be a sign of understanding and respect for others. It's about recognizing that we don't always need to speak, that sometimes silence can be more powerful and respectful than words. In this way, silence is not just about avoiding trouble or conflict, but also about showing kindness, respect, and understanding to others. The Bible also connects silence with trust in God. In Psalm 46:10, it says, "Be still, and know that I am God: I will be exalted among the heathen, I will be exalted in the earth." This verse invites us to be still, to be silent, and to trust in God's power and presence. Silence, in this sense, is a way of demonstrating our faith in God, of acknowledging that we don't always need to have the answers or to speak, but that we can trust in God's plan and His timing. Silence can also be a way of finding peace and rest in God. In Isaiah 30:15, it says, "For thus saith the Lord God, the Holy One of Israel; In returning and rest shall ye be saved; in quietness and in confidence shall be your strength: and ye would not." This verse shows that quietness, or silence, is linked with strength and salvation. It suggests that in silence and trust in God, we can find strength and peace. Silence is not just about refraining from speaking; it's about creating space for God in our lives, about finding rest and strength in Him. In Exodus 14:14, it says, "The Lord shall fight for you, and ye shall hold your peace." This verse reminds us that sometimes the best thing we can do is to remain silent and trust that God will take care of the situation. By holding our peace, by remaining silent, we show our faith in God's ability to protect us and to work things out for our good. Throughout the Bible, silence is portrayed as a sacred and powerful practice, one that can protect us, guard our soul, and help us to avoid unnecessary trouble. It's a way of practicing self-control, of demonstrating wisdom, and of showing respect and humility to others. Silence allows us to listen more, to understand better, and to respond in a way that promotes peace rather than conflict. It's about recognizing the power of our words and choosing to use them carefully and thoughtfully. In a noisy world, the Bible's teachings on silence offer a different way of living, one that encourages us to slow down, to be more mindful of our speech, and to find strength and peace in quietness and trust in God. Silence is not just the absence of words; it is a powerful and intentional practice that can lead to greater wisdom, understanding, and spiritual growth. The Bible, especially in the King James Version, teaches us that silence speaks volumes, and sometimes the most powerful thing we can do is to hold our peace and trust in God.

Chapter 3 - Developing Patience

The sacred art of silence is a powerful concept in the Bible, especially in the King James Version (KJV), where it is often connected to patience and the wisdom of knowing when to speak and when to keep silent. One of the most important verses that teach us about the significance of silence and patience is found in Ecclesiastes 3:7, which says, "A time to rend, and a time to sew; a time to keep silence, and a time to speak." This verse is part of a larger passage that talks about the different seasons and times in life for various actions, suggesting that there is an appropriate time for everything, including silence. The Bible, in this verse, emphasizes that silence is not just the absence of speech but an intentional choice that requires wisdom and patience. Knowing when to keep silent and when to speak is a critical part of living wisely and navigating the complexities of life. Silence teaches us to be patient, to wait for the right moment, and to understand that not every situation requires a verbal response. In fact, sometimes, the most powerful response we can give is no response at all, allowing the situation to unfold without adding unnecessary words that could complicate or escalate matters. The Bible teaches that patience, which is closely linked with silence, is a virtue that can help us avoid conflict and make better decisions. By practicing silence, we learn to control our impulses and to think before we speak, which can prevent us from saying things we might later regret. In Proverbs 10:19, it says, "In the multitude of words there wanteth not sin: but he that refraineth his lips is wise." This verse reminds us that talking too much can lead to sin, while being silent and thoughtful can be a sign of wisdom. Silence, therefore, is not just about refraining from speaking but about exercising patience and wisdom in our communication. Patience is essential in many aspects of life, and silence is a key part of developing this virtue. The Bible also connects silence with spiritual growth, showing that by being patient and waiting on God, we can grow stronger in our faith. In Lamentations 3:26, it says, "It is good that a man should both hope and quietly wait for the salvation of the Lord." This verse suggests that silence and patience go hand in hand, and that by quietly waiting on the Lord, we demonstrate our trust in His timing and His plan for our lives. Silence, in this context, is a way of showing our faith and reliance on God, knowing that He will act in His perfect time. The Bible also highlights the importance of patience and silence in avoiding unnecessary conflicts. In Proverbs 15:1, it says, "A soft answer turneth away wrath: but grievous words stir up anger." This verse shows that how we respond to others can either calm a situation or make it worse. Sometimes, the best way to avoid conflict is to remain silent or to respond gently, demonstrating patience and self-control. Silence gives us the space to think before we speak, to consider the impact of our words, and to choose a response that promotes peace rather than anger. In James 1:19, we are instructed, "Wherefore, my beloved brethren, let every man be swift to hear, slow to speak, slow to wrath." This verse teaches us the importance of listening more and speaking less, which requires patience and self-control. By being slow to speak, we give ourselves time to listen, to understand, and to respond in a way that is thoughtful and wise. Silence, in this sense, is not just about not talking but about being patient and deliberate in our communication. The Bible also connects silence with humility and the recognition that we do not always have the answers. In Proverbs 11:12, it says, "He that is void of wisdom despiseth his neighbour: but a man of understanding holdeth his peace." This verse suggests that holding our peace, or remaining silent, can be a sign of understanding and respect for others. It's about acknowledging that we don't always need to speak, that sometimes silence can be more powerful and respectful than words. In this way, silence is a demonstration of humility, patience, and wisdom, recognizing that there are times when it is better to listen and observe rather than to speak. The Bible's teachings on silence also remind us of the importance of timing in our communication. In Ecclesiastes 3:7, where it says there is "a time to keep silence, and a time to speak," we are reminded that timing is crucial in all aspects of life, including our speech. Knowing when to speak and when to remain silent is a skill that requires patience and discernment. It's about understanding the context, the people involved, and the potential consequences of our words. Silence gives us the opportunity to consider all these factors before we speak, ensuring that our words are timely, appropriate, and effective. The Bible also shows us that silence can be a way of demonstrating our trust in God's timing. In Psalm 46:10, it says, "Be still, and know that I am God." This verse invites us to be still, to be silent, and to trust in God's power and presence. Silence, in this context, is about being patient and waiting on God, knowing that He is in control and that He will act in His perfect time. By practicing silence, we demonstrate our faith and our trust in God's timing, recognizing that we do not always need to speak or act but that sometimes the best thing we can do is to wait patiently on the Lord. Silence is also a way of finding peace and rest in God. In Isaiah 30:15, it says, "For thus saith the Lord God, the Holy One of Israel; In returning and rest shall ye be saved; in quietness and in confidence shall be your strength: and ye would not." This verse shows that quietness, or silence, is linked with strength and salvation. It suggests that in silence and trust in God, we can find strength and peace. Silence, therefore, is not just about refraining from speaking; it's about creating space for God in our lives, about finding rest and strength in Him. The Bible also connects silence with self-control, which is closely related to patience. In Proverbs 13:3, it says, "He that keepeth his mouth keepeth his life: but he that openeth wide his lips shall have destruction." This verse highlights the importance of controlling our speech and being patient in our communication. Silence, in this context, is about exercising self-control and choosing to speak only when it is necessary and appropriate. It's about being patient and waiting for the right moment to speak, ensuring that our words are measured and thoughtful. In the Bible, silence is also portrayed as a way of demonstrating our faith in God's plan and timing. In Exodus 14:14, it says, "The Lord shall fight for you, and ye shall hold your peace." This verse reminds us that sometimes the best thing we can do is to remain silent and trust that God will take care of the situation. By holding our peace, by remaining silent, we show our faith in God's ability to protect us and to work things out for our good. Silence, therefore, is a way of demonstrating patience, trust, and reliance on God, knowing that He is in control and that He will act in His perfect time. Throughout the Bible, silence is portrayed as a sacred and powerful practice, one that is closely linked with patience, wisdom, and spiritual growth. Silence teaches us to be patient, to wait for the right moment, and to understand that not every situation requires a verbal response. It's about exercising self-control, showing humility, and demonstrating our faith in God's plan and timing. Silence gives us the space to think before we speak, to consider the impact of our words, and to choose a response that is thoughtful, measured, and appropriate. In a world that is often noisy and chaotic, the Bible's teachings on silence offer a different way of living, one that encourages us to slow down, to be more mindful of our words, and to find strength and peace in quietness and trust in God. Silence is not just the absence of words; it is a powerful and intentional practice that can lead to greater wisdom, understanding, and spiritual growth. The Bible, especially in the King James Version, teaches us that silence speaks volumes, and sometimes the most powerful thing we can do is to hold our peace, be patient, and trust in God's timing. By embracing the sacred art of silence, we can learn to navigate the complexities of life with wisdom, patience, and grace, knowing that there is a time for everything, including a time to keep silence and a time to speak.

Chapter 4 - Deepening Spiritual Reflection

Silence is a powerful and sacred practice that is deeply woven into the fabric of Scripture, particularly in the King James Version (KJV) of the Bible. One of the profound ways silence speaks to us in the Bible is through the practice of spiritual reflection. The Bible often highlights the importance of taking time to be still, to be quiet, and to reflect on our spiritual lives, and one of the key verses that illustrates this is found in Lamentations 3:26, which says, "It is good that a man should both hope and quietly wait for the salvation of the Lord." This verse captures the essence of what it means to use silence as a tool for spiritual reflection. It reminds us that there is great value in waiting quietly on the Lord, in being patient and still as we seek His presence and guidance. Silence provides the necessary space for us to focus on our relationship with God, to listen for His voice, and to reflect on His word and His will for our lives.

Spiritual reflection is an essential aspect of the Christian walk, and silence plays a crucial role in making this reflection possible. In the hustle and bustle of everyday life, it can be challenging to find the time and space to truly reflect on our spiritual journey. However, the Bible teaches us that taking time for silence is not just important, but necessary for our spiritual growth and well-being. Silence allows us to shut out the distractions of the world and to turn our attention fully to God. It is in these quiet moments that we can meditate on His word, consider His teachings, and examine our own hearts and lives in light of His truth.

The Bible is full of examples of individuals who used silence as a means of drawing closer to God. For example, in Psalm 46:10, we are instructed, "Be still, and know that I am God." This verse encourages us to embrace stillness and silence as a way of coming to a deeper understanding of who God is. It is in the quiet that we can truly know God, to experience His presence and His power in a way that is often difficult to do in the midst of noise and activity. Silence, therefore, becomes a pathway to greater spiritual insight and a more intimate relationship with the Lord.

Another key aspect of spiritual reflection is the practice of waiting on the Lord, which is closely linked with silence. In Isaiah 40:31, it says, "But they that wait upon the Lord shall renew their strength; they shall mount up with wings as eagles; they shall run, and not be weary; and they shall walk, and not faint." This verse speaks to the strength and renewal that comes from waiting on God, from taking the time to be still and to wait for His guidance and direction. Silence allows us to wait patiently for the Lord, to trust in His timing and His plan, and to find strength and peace in His presence. In these moments of silence and waiting, we are reminded that our hope is in the Lord, and that He is faithful to those who seek Him.

The Bible also teaches us that silence is a way of humbling ourselves before God. In Habakkuk 2:20, it says, "But the Lord is in his holy temple: let all the earth keep silence before him." This verse calls us to silence as a sign of reverence and awe for the Lord. It reminds us that in the presence of God, there is no need for words, only a deep sense of respect and worship. Silence, in this context, is a way of acknowledging God's greatness and our own need for His mercy and grace. It is in these moments of quiet reverence that we can truly reflect on God's holiness and our place in His creation.

Spiritual reflection through silence is also about creating space for God to speak to us. In 1 Kings 19:12, the prophet Elijah experiences God not in the wind, the earthquake, or the fire, but in a "still small voice." This passage illustrates that God's voice is often heard in the silence, in the quiet moments when we are still and attentive to His presence. Silence, therefore, becomes a way of tuning our hearts and minds to the voice of God, of making ourselves available to hear what

He has to say to us. It is in these quiet times of reflection that we can receive guidance, encouragement, and comfort from the Lord.

The Bible also connects silence with the idea of rest and renewal. In Matthew 11:28, Jesus invites us, saying, "Come unto me, all ye that labour and are heavy laden, and I will give you rest." While this verse does not explicitly mention silence, the concept of rest is closely tied to the idea of finding peace and renewal in the presence of God. Silence allows us to enter into that rest, to lay aside our burdens and to find refreshment for our souls. It is in these moments of quiet reflection that we can experience the peace that passes all understanding, the peace that only God can give.

Furthermore, silence is a way of focusing on God's word and allowing it to penetrate our hearts. In Psalm 119:15, the psalmist declares, "I will meditate in thy precepts, and have respect unto thy ways." Meditation, which involves silent reflection on God's word, is a key practice in the spiritual life. It allows us to internalize the teachings of Scripture, to consider how they apply to our lives, and to allow God's truth to transform us from the inside out. Silence creates the space for this kind of deep, meaningful reflection, helping us to grow in our understanding of God's will and His ways.

In addition to meditation, silence is also connected with prayer. In Romans 8:26, it says, "Likewise the Spirit also helpeth our infirmities: for we know not what we should pray for as we ought: but the Spirit itself maketh intercession for us with groanings which cannot be uttered." This verse suggests that there are times when words are not enough, when our prayers go beyond what we can express in speech. In these moments, silence becomes a form of prayer, a way of opening our hearts to God and allowing the Holy Spirit to intercede on our behalf. Silence, in prayer, is about trusting that God knows our needs even when we cannot put them into words, and about resting in His presence as we wait for His response.

Silence also provides an opportunity for self-examination and repentance. In Psalm 4:4, we are instructed, "Stand in awe, and sin not: commune with your own heart upon your bed, and be still." This verse encourages us to take time for quiet reflection, to examine our hearts and to consider our actions in light of God's holiness. Silence allows us to confront our sins, to seek God's forgiveness, and to make the necessary changes in our lives. It is in these moments of silent reflection that we can experience the cleansing and renewal that comes from true repentance.

Moreover, silence is a way of practicing gratitude and contentment. In Philippians 4:11, Paul writes, "Not that I speak in respect of want: for I have learned, in whatsoever state I am, therewith to be content." While this verse does not directly mention silence, the practice of contentment often involves taking time to reflect on our blessings and to give thanks to God for His provision. Silence provides the space for this kind of reflection, helping us to cultivate a heart of gratitude and to find contentment in the Lord's goodness.

Silence is also about waiting for God's justice and trusting in His timing. In Psalm 37:7, it says, "Rest in the Lord, and wait patiently for him: fret not thyself because of him who prospereth in his way, because of the man who bringeth wicked devices to pass." This verse encourages us to be patient and to trust that God will bring about justice in His own time. Silence, in this context, is about resisting the urge to take matters into our own hands and instead waiting quietly for God to act. It is about trusting that God's timing is perfect and that He will set things right in His own way.

In addition to waiting on God's justice, silence is also a way of preparing ourselves for His return. In Revelation 8:1, it says, "And when he had opened the seventh seal, there was silence in heaven about the space of half an hour." This verse speaks of a profound silence in heaven as the final judgments are about to be revealed. This silence is a moment of awe and anticipation, a time of preparation for what is to come. In our own lives, silence can be a way of preparing our hearts for the return of Christ, of reflecting on His promises and living in readiness for His coming.

Finally, silence is a way of experiencing the peace of God. In John 14:27, Jesus says, "Peace I leave with you, my peace I give unto you: not as the world giveth, give I unto you. Let not your heart be troubled, neither let it be afraid." This peace, which surpasses all understanding, is often found in the quiet moments of life, in the times when we set aside the noise and distractions of the world and focus on the presence of God. Silence allows us to enter into this peace, to rest in the assurance of God's love and care, and to find comfort in His presence.

Throughout the Bible, silence is portrayed as a sacred and powerful practice, one that is essential for spiritual reflection and growth. It is in the quiet moments of life that we can draw closer to God, reflect on His word, and seek His guidance and direction. Silence provides the space for us to meditate on God's teachings, to pray, to repent, and to give thanks. It is a way of demonstrating our trust in God's timing and His plan, of waiting patiently for His justice and His return. Silence allows us to experience the peace of God, to rest in His presence, and to find strength and renewal in Him. In a world

that is often noisy and chaotic, the Bible's teachings on silence offer a different way of living, one that encourages us to slow down, to be still, and to focus on our relationship with God. The sacred art of silence is a timeless and valuable practice that can lead to greater wisdom, understanding, and spiritual depth. The Bible, especially in the King James Version, teaches us that silence is not just the absence of words, but a powerful and intentional practice that can transform our lives and deepen our connection with the Lord. By embracing the sacred art of silence, we can learn to listen for God's voice, to reflect on His word, and to grow in our faith and our love for Him.

Chapter 5 - Dodging Sin

Silence is a profound and sacred concept in the Bible, and it plays a crucial role in helping us to live a life that is pleasing to God. The King James Version (KJV) of the Bible emphasizes the importance of silence as a way to prevent sin, guiding us to use our words wisely and to understand that what we say can have a significant impact on our spiritual lives. One of the key verses that teaches us about the power of silence in preventing sin is found in Proverbs 10:19, which says, "In the multitude of words there wanteth not sin: but he that refraineth his lips is wise." This verse highlights a timeless truth: the more we talk, the more likely we are to say something wrong or harmful, leading to sin. In contrast, those who choose to be silent and think carefully before they speak are considered wise. This wisdom is not just about avoiding trouble in the moment, but about understanding the deeper spiritual implications of our words.

The Bible often warns us about the dangers of excessive talking. Words, once spoken, cannot be taken back, and they have the power to build up or tear down, to heal or to harm. When we speak without thinking, we risk saying things that can lead to gossip, slander, lying, and other forms of sinful behavior. Gossip, in particular, is a common sin that is fueled by careless talk. In Proverbs 16:28, it says, "A froward man soweth strife: and a whisperer separateth chief friends." Gossip and slander can destroy relationships, spread falsehoods, and create division among people. The Bible teaches us that by restraining our speech, by choosing silence over the impulse to talk, we can avoid falling into these traps of sin.

Moreover, the Bible emphasizes that restraint in speech is a mark of wisdom. In Proverbs 17:27-28, it says, "He that hath knowledge spareth his words: and a man of understanding is of an excellent spirit. Even a fool, when he holdeth his peace, is counted wise: and he that shutteth his lips is esteemed a man of understanding." These verses remind us that true wisdom is often demonstrated not by how much we say, but by how much we refrain from saying. Silence, in this context, is not a sign of weakness or ignorance, but of self-control and discernment. It takes wisdom to know when to speak and when to remain silent, and those who master this art are considered wise in the eyes of God.

Silence also helps us to avoid the sin of lying. The Bible is clear that lying is a sin that God detests. In Proverbs 12:22, it says, "Lying lips are abomination to the Lord: but they that deal truly are his delight." When we speak without thinking, we are more likely to exaggerate, distort the truth, or even lie outright. By practicing silence and thinking carefully before we speak, we can avoid the temptation to lie and instead speak truthfully and honestly. Silence, therefore, becomes a tool for maintaining integrity and righteousness in our lives.

In addition to preventing gossip and lying, silence can also help us avoid the sin of anger. In James 1:19, we are instructed, "Wherefore, my beloved brethren, let every man be swift to hear, slow to speak, slow to wrath." This verse connects the act of speaking with the emotion of anger, suggesting that by being slow to speak, we can also be slow to anger. When we take the time to be silent and think before we respond, we are less likely to react in anger and say things that we might later regret. Silence gives us the space to calm down, to consider our words carefully, and to choose a response that is measured and wise. In this way, silence helps us to avoid the sin of anger and to promote peace in our relationships.

The Bible also teaches us that silence can prevent the sin of boasting. In Proverbs 27:2, it says, "Let another man praise thee, and not thine own mouth; a stranger, and not thine own lips." Boasting, or speaking pridefully about ourselves, is a form of sinful behavior that can lead to arrogance and self-exaltation. By choosing to be silent instead of boasting, we demonstrate humility and acknowledge that all our accomplishments are by God's grace and not by our own doing. Silence, therefore, becomes a way of practicing humility and avoiding the sin of pride.

Furthermore, silence can help us avoid the sin of judgment and criticism. In Matthew 7:1-2, Jesus warns, "Judge not, that ye be not judged. For with what judgment ye judge, ye shall be judged: and with what measure ye mete, it shall be measured to you again." When we speak too quickly, we are often tempted to judge others, to criticize their actions, and to make harsh comments that can hurt and condemn. Silence allows us to pause, to refrain from passing judgment, and to consider the impact of our words. It gives us the opportunity to show grace and understanding instead of rushing to criticize. In this way, silence helps us to avoid the sin of judgment and to cultivate a spirit of compassion and mercy.

Silence also plays a role in preventing the sin of blasphemy and taking the Lord's name in vain. In Exodus 20:7, one of the Ten Commandments instructs, "Thou shalt not take the name of the Lord thy God in vain; for the Lord will not hold him guiltless that taketh his name in vain." When we speak without thinking, especially in moments of frustration or anger, we may be tempted to use God's name carelessly or inappropriately. By practicing silence, we can avoid this serious sin and ensure that we use God's name with the reverence and respect it deserves.

The Bible also warns us about the sin of false teaching and leading others astray with our words. In 2 Timothy 2:16-17, it says, "But shun profane and vain babblings: for they will increase unto more ungodliness. And their word will eat as doth a canker." False teaching and spreading incorrect doctrine can have devastating effects on others' faith and spiritual lives. By choosing to be silent when we are unsure of the truth, and by carefully considering our words before we speak, we can avoid leading others astray and causing harm with our speech. Silence, in this context, is a way of protecting ourselves and others from the sin of false teaching.

Silence is also a way to prevent the sin of creating strife and discord among people. In Proverbs 6:16-19, it lists the things that the Lord hates, and among them is "he that soweth discord among brethren." When we speak carelessly, we risk creating misunderstandings, spreading rumors, and causing divisions within the community. Silence helps us to avoid this sin by encouraging us to think carefully before we speak, to ensure that our words promote unity and peace rather than division and strife.

In addition to these specific sins, the Bible teaches that silence can prevent the general sin of speaking in a way that is unloving or unkind. In Ephesians 4:29, it says, "Let no corrupt communication proceed out of your mouth, but that which is good to the use of edifying, that it may minister grace unto the hearers." This verse reminds us that our words should be used to build others up, to encourage and support them, rather than to tear them down. When we are silent, we give ourselves time to consider whether our words are kind, loving, and edifying. Silence helps us to avoid the sin of speaking harshly or unkindly and instead encourages us to use our words to bless and uplift others.

Moreover, the Bible connects silence with the idea of being slow to speak and quick to listen. In Proverbs 18:13, it says, "He that answereth a matter before he heareth it, it is folly and shame unto him." This verse teaches that speaking without listening is foolish and can lead to misunderstandings and sin. Silence allows us to listen more carefully, to understand the situation fully before we respond, and to avoid the sin of speaking out of turn or without proper knowledge. By being silent and listening first, we show wisdom and avoid the folly and shame that comes from speaking prematurely.

The Bible also emphasizes that silence can prevent the sin of provoking others to anger. In Proverbs 15:1, it says, "A soft answer turneth away wrath: but grievous words stir up anger." This verse teaches that our words have the power to either calm a situation or make it worse. When we choose to be silent instead of responding with harsh or grievous words, we prevent the sin of provoking anger and instead promote peace and understanding. Silence, therefore, becomes a way of diffusing tense situations and avoiding the sin of stirring up conflict.

Silence is also associated with the prevention of the sin of disrespecting authority. In Ecclesiastes 10:20, it says, "Curse not the king, no not in thy thought; and curse not the rich in thy bedchamber: for a bird of the air shall carry the voice, and that which hath wings shall tell the matter." This verse warns us that even private words spoken against those in authority can become public and lead to trouble. By practicing silence and refraining from speaking ill of others, especially those in positions of authority, we can avoid the sin of disrespect and the consequences that come with it.

Furthermore, silence can prevent the sin of impatience and complaining. In Philippians 2:14, it says, "Do all things without murmurings and disputings." Complaining and grumbling are sins that often arise from impatience and dissatisfaction. Silence helps us to control these impulses, to accept our circumstances with grace, and to avoid the sin of complaining. By choosing to be silent instead

of voicing our complaints, we demonstrate patience and trust in God's plan, knowing that He is in control and that He will provide for our needs.

The Bible also teaches that silence can prevent the sin of swearing and making rash vows. In Matthew 5:34-37, Jesus instructs, "But I say unto you, Swear not at all; neither by heaven; for it is God's throne: Nor by the earth; for it is his footstool: neither by Jerusalem; for it is the city of the great King. Neither shalt thou swear by thy head, because thou canst not make one hair white or black. But let your communication be, Yea, yea; Nay, nay: for whatsoever is more than these cometh of evil." This passage teaches that we should avoid making rash vows or swearing by anything, as this can lead to sin. Silence, in this context, is about being careful with our words, avoiding the temptation to make promises or commitments that we cannot keep, and instead letting our simple yes or no be sufficient.

Finally, silence can prevent the sin of speaking in a way that dishonors God. In Psalm 19:14, it says, "Let the words of my mouth, and the meditation of my heart, be acceptable in thy sight, O Lord, my strength, and my redeemer." This verse is a prayer that our words and thoughts would be pleasing to God. By practicing silence and being mindful of what we say, we can ensure that our speech honors God and reflects His love and truth. Silence helps us to avoid the sin of speaking in a way that is dishonoring or displeasing to God and instead encourages us to use our words to glorify Him.

Throughout the Bible, silence is portrayed as a sacred and powerful practice that can help us to live a life free from sin. By choosing to be silent, we can avoid the sins of gossip, lying, anger, boasting, judgment, blasphemy, false teaching, strife, unkind speech, premature speech, provoking anger, disrespect, complaining, rash vows, and dishonoring God. Silence is a way of demonstrating wisdom, self-control, humility, and respect for others and for God. It allows us to think carefully before we speak, to listen more than we talk, and to ensure that our words are loving, kind, and edifying. In a world where words are often spoken carelessly and without thought, the Bible's teachings on silence offer a different way of living, one that encourages us to be mindful of our speech and to use our words to build up rather than to tear down. The sacred art of silence is a timeless and valuable practice that can help us to prevent sin, to grow in wisdom and understanding, and to live a life that is pleasing to God. The Bible, especially in the King James Version, teaches us that silence is not just the absence of words, but a powerful and intentional practice that can transform our lives and help us to avoid the many pitfalls of sinful speech. By embracing the sacred art of silence, we can learn to speak only when necessary, to use our words wisely, and to live a life that reflects the love and truth of God.

Chapter 6 - Dedicating to Peace

Silence is a profound and sacred practice in the Bible, especially in the King James Version (KJV), where it is closely linked with cultivating peace. The Bible teaches us that silence is not just the absence of words but a powerful tool that can foster peace in our hearts, our relationships, and our communities. One of the key verses that illustrates the importance of silence in cultivating peace is found in James 1:19, which says, "Wherefore, my beloved brethren, let every man be swift to hear, slow to speak, slow to wrath." This verse highlights the wisdom of being quick to listen and slow to speak, emphasizing that silence can help us avoid anger and promote calm, peaceful interactions with others. By practicing silence, we give ourselves the space to listen carefully, to understand fully, and to respond thoughtfully, rather than reacting hastily or out of anger. This restraint in speech is a key aspect of living peacefully and wisely.

The Bible often connects the idea of silence with the cultivation of peace. In Proverbs 15:1, it says, "A soft answer turneth away wrath: but grievous words stir up anger." This verse reminds us that our words have the power to either calm a situation or make it worse. By choosing to respond with gentle, soft words—or by choosing to remain silent—we can turn away wrath and prevent conflicts from escalating. Silence, in this context, is a way of defusing tension and avoiding unnecessary arguments. It allows us to maintain peace in our interactions with others, showing that we value harmony over the need to be heard or to have the last word.

Moreover, the Bible teaches us that silence can be a way of showing respect and understanding. In Proverbs 17:27-28, it says, "He that hath knowledge spareth his words: and a man of understanding is of an excellent spirit. Even a fool, when he holdeth his peace, is counted wise: and he that shutteth his lips is esteemed a man of understanding." These verses suggest that those who are wise and understanding are careful with their words, choosing to speak only when necessary. Silence, in this sense, is a mark of wisdom and maturity. It shows that we are more interested in understanding others and maintaining peace than in winning arguments or proving ourselves right. By cultivating silence, we cultivate an attitude of respect and humility, which in turn fosters peaceful relationships.

Silence also helps us to avoid the sin of gossip, which is often a source of conflict and division. In Proverbs 16:28, it says, "A froward man soweth strife: and a whisperer separateth chief friends." Gossip and slander can destroy relationships and create discord among people. By choosing to be silent and refraining from speaking negatively about others, we prevent the spread of harmful words and protect the peace within our communities. Silence, therefore, becomes a tool for preserving harmony and unity, ensuring that our words do not contribute to strife or division.

In addition to preventing gossip, silence also helps us to avoid the sin of anger, which can easily disrupt peace. In Ecclesiastes 7:9, it says, "Be not hasty in thy spirit to be angry: for anger resteth in the bosom of fools." This verse teaches that anger is often the result of hasty, unconsidered reactions. When we speak out of anger, we are more likely to say things that hurt others and cause conflict. Silence, on the other hand, gives us the time to calm down, to think about our response, and to choose words that promote peace rather than anger. By being slow to speak and slow to anger, we create an environment of calm and understanding, where peace can flourish.

The Bible also connects silence with the idea of patience, which is essential for cultivating peace. In Proverbs 14:29, it says, "He that is slow to wrath is of great understanding: but he that is hasty of spirit exalteth folly." This verse emphasizes the value of being patient and deliberate in our responses, rather than reacting impulsively. Silence helps us to practice this patience, allowing us to consider the situation carefully before we speak or act. It helps us to avoid rash decisions and hasty words that can lead to conflict. By cultivating silence, we cultivate patience, which in turn fosters peace in our interactions with others.

Silence is also a way of creating space for reflection and self-examination, which are important for maintaining peace in our hearts and relationships. In Psalm 4:4, it says, "Stand in awe, and sin not: commune with your own heart upon your bed, and be still." This verse encourages us to take time for quiet reflection, to examine our own hearts, and to be still before the Lord. Silence allows us to look inward, to consider our own actions and attitudes, and to make the necessary changes to live more peacefully. It is in these moments of silence and reflection that we can find the peace that comes from knowing we are walking in the ways of the Lord.

The Bible also teaches that silence can be a way of avoiding unnecessary conflicts and disputes. In Proverbs 17:14, it says, "The beginning of strife is as when one letteth out water: therefore leave off contention, before it be meddled with." This verse suggests that once a conflict begins, it can quickly escalate, like water being released from a dam. Silence helps us to "leave off contention," to avoid engaging in arguments that could lead to strife. By choosing to remain silent instead of responding to provocation, we prevent conflicts from starting and maintain peace in our relationships.

In addition to preventing conflict, silence can also be a way of promoting peace by allowing us to listen more effectively. In Proverbs 18:13, it says, "He that answereth a matter before he heareth it, it is folly and shame unto him." This verse teaches that speaking without listening is foolish and can lead to misunderstandings and conflict. Silence allows us to listen fully and attentively to others, to understand their perspective before we respond. By listening more and speaking less, we show respect for others' views and create an environment where peaceful, constructive dialogue can take place.

Silence is also connected with the idea of being slow to judgment, which is essential for maintaining peace in our relationships. In

Matthew 7:1-2, Jesus warns, "Judge not, that ye be not judged. For with what judgment ye judge, ye shall be judged: and with what measure ye mete, it shall be measured to you again." When we are quick to judge others, we often create conflict and division. Silence helps us to refrain from making hasty judgments, to take the time to understand the full situation before we speak. By being slow to judge and quick to listen, we foster an environment of grace and understanding, where peace can thrive.

The Bible also teaches that silence can be a way of avoiding unnecessary criticism and negative speech, which can disrupt peace. In Ephesians 4:29, it says, "Let no corrupt communication proceed out of your mouth, but that which is good to the use of edifying, that it may minister grace unto the hearers." This verse encourages us to use our words to build others up, rather than to tear them down. Silence helps us to control our speech, to ensure that our words are kind, loving, and edifying. By choosing to be silent rather than speaking negatively, we promote peace and harmony in our relationships.

Furthermore, silence can help us to avoid the sin of boasting, which can create tension and conflict. In Proverbs 27:2, it says, "Let another man praise thee, and not thine own mouth; a stranger, and not thine own lips." Boasting, or speaking pridefully about ourselves, can lead to envy, jealousy, and strife. By choosing to be silent instead of boasting, we demonstrate humility and promote peace in our interactions with others. Silence, in this context, is a way of practicing modesty and ensuring that our words do not create unnecessary conflict or competition.

The Bible also connects silence with the practice of forgiveness, which is essential for maintaining peace. In Colossians 3:13, it says, "Forbearing one another, and forgiving one another, if any man have a quarrel against any: even as Christ forgave you, so also do ye." Forgiveness often requires us to be silent, to refrain from speaking words of anger or resentment, and instead to offer grace and understanding. Silence helps us to let go of grudges, to forgive others, and to restore peace in our relationships.

In addition to promoting forgiveness, silence can also be a way of showing respect for others' opinions and feelings. In Romans 14:19, it says, "Let us therefore follow after the things which make for peace, and things wherewith one may edify another." This verse encourages us to seek peace in our interactions with others, to focus on building up rather than tearing down. Silence helps us to practice this by allowing us to listen respectfully to others, to consider their feelings and perspectives, and to respond in a way that promotes peace and understanding.

Silence is also a way of practicing self-control, which is essential for cultivating peace. In Proverbs 25:28, it says, "He that hath no rule over his own spirit is like a city that is broken down, and without walls." This verse teaches that without self-control, we are vulnerable to all kinds of negative influences, including anger, jealousy, and strife. Silence helps us to practice self-control, to rule over our own spirit, and to ensure that our words and actions promote peace rather than conflict. By cultivating silence, we cultivate self-control, which in turn fosters peace in our hearts and our relationships.

The Bible also teaches that silence can be a way of demonstrating our trust in God's plan and timing, which is essential for maintaining peace. In Psalm 46:10, it says, "Be still,

and know that I am God." This verse encourages us to be still, to be silent, and to trust in God's sovereignty and wisdom. Silence helps us to let go of our need to control every situation, to trust that God is in control, and to find peace in His presence. By being silent and still before the Lord, we cultivate a deep sense of peace and contentment, knowing that He is working all things together for our good.

In addition to promoting trust in God, silence can also be a way of avoiding the sin of provoking others to anger. In Proverbs 15:18, it says, "A wrathful man stirreth up strife: but he that is slow to anger appeaseth strife." This verse teaches that anger and hasty speech can stir up conflict, while patience and restraint can calm it. Silence helps us to avoid provoking others, to choose words that promote peace rather than strife, and to create an environment of calm and understanding. By being slow to speak and slow to anger, we cultivate peace in our relationships and avoid the sin of stirring up conflict.

Silence is also associated with the practice of contentment, which is essential for maintaining peace in our hearts. In Philippians 4:11, Paul writes, "Not that I speak in respect of want: for I have learned, in whatsoever state I am, therewith to be content." Contentment often involves being silent, accepting our circumstances with grace, and finding peace in the knowledge that God is in control. Silence helps us to practice contentment, to focus on our blessings rather than our wants, and to cultivate a heart of gratitude and peace.

The Bible also connects silence with the idea of being slow to speak and quick to listen, which is essential for maintaining peace in our interactions with others. In Proverbs 18:2, it says, "A fool hath no delight in understanding, but that his heart may discover itself." This verse teaches that those who are quick to speak and slow to listen are often more interested in expressing their own opinions than in understanding others. Silence helps us to avoid this folly, to listen carefully to others, and to seek understanding before we speak. By being quick to listen and slow to speak, we promote peace and understanding in our relationships.

In addition to promoting understanding, silence can also be a way of avoiding the sin of speaking rashly, which can disrupt peace. In Proverbs 29:20, it says, "Seest thou a man that is hasty in his words? there is more hope of a fool than of him." This verse teaches that hasty speech is often foolish and can lead to regret. Silence helps us to avoid speaking rashly, to think carefully before we speak, and to choose words that promote peace rather than conflict. By being slow to speak, we cultivate wisdom and avoid the folly of rash words.

The Bible also teaches that silence can be a way of avoiding unnecessary disputes, which can disrupt peace. In 2 Timothy 2:23-24, it says, "But foolish and unlearned questions avoid, knowing that they do gender strifes. And the servant of the Lord must not strive; but be gentle unto all men, apt to teach, patient." This verse encourages us to avoid engaging in disputes over trivial matters, which can lead to strife. Silence helps us to avoid these unnecessary arguments, to focus on what is truly important, and to promote peace in our interactions with others.

Finally, silence is a way of experiencing the peace of God in our hearts. In John 14:27, Jesus says, "Peace I leave with you, my peace I give unto you: not as the world giveth, give I unto you. Let not your heart be troubled, neither let it be afraid." This peace, which surpasses all understanding, is often found in the quiet moments of life, in the times when we set aside the noise and distractions of the world and focus on the presence of God. Silence allows us to enter into this peace, to rest in the assurance of God's love and care, and to find comfort in His presence.

Throughout the Bible, silence is portrayed as a sacred and powerful practice that is essential for cultivating peace. By choosing to be silent, we can avoid the sins of gossip, anger, boasting, judgment, criticism, and rash speech. Silence helps us to listen more, to understand better, and to respond in a way that promotes peace and harmony in our relationships. It is a way of practicing self-control, patience, humility, and respect for others and for God. Silence allows us to create space for reflection, self-examination, and prayer, to cultivate contentment, and to experience the peace of God in our hearts. In a world that is often noisy and chaotic, the Bible's teachings on silence offer a different way of living, one that encourages us to be mindful of our words and to use our speech to build up rather than to tear down. The sacred art of silence is a timeless and valuable practice that can help us to cultivate peace in our hearts, our relationships, and our communities. The Bible, especially in the King James Version, teaches us that silence is not just the absence of words, but a powerful and intentional practice that can transform our lives and help us to live in peace with God and with others. By embracing the sacred art of silence, we can learn to speak only when necessary, to use our words wisely, and to cultivate a spirit of peace and harmony in all that we do.

Chapter 7 - Deepening Prayer Life

Silence is a sacred and profound practice deeply rooted in Scripture, and it plays a crucial role in deepening our prayer life. The Bible, particularly in the King James Version (KJV), speaks of silence as an essential aspect of communion with God, where stillness before the Lord allows us to become more aware of His presence and sovereignty. One of the most powerful verses that highlights the importance of silence in our spiritual life is found in Psalm 46:10, which says, "Be still, and know that I am God: I will be exalted among the heathen, I will be exalted in the earth." This verse captures the essence of how silence can deepen our prayer life. It calls us to be still, to cease from our busyness and distractions, and to focus entirely on God, recognizing His greatness and His authority over all things. Silence, in this context, is not just about the absence of noise but about creating a space where we can encounter God in a more intimate and profound way.

In our daily lives, we are often surrounded by noise and constant activity, which can make it difficult to hear God's voice. The Bible teaches that silence is a powerful tool that allows us to cut through the noise and distractions of the world, bringing us into a place where we can truly connect with God in prayer. Silence helps us to quiet our minds and hearts, making room for the Holy Spirit to move within us and speak to us. It is in these moments of stillness that we can hear the gentle whispers of God's voice, guiding us, comforting us, and drawing us closer to Him.

The Bible emphasizes the importance of silence in prayer and meditation as a means of experiencing God's presence more fully. In 1 Kings 19:11-12, we read about the prophet Elijah, who encounters God not in the powerful wind, earthquake, or fire, but in a "still small voice." This passage illustrates that God's voice is often heard in the quiet, in the silence where we are most attuned to His presence. By embracing silence in our prayer life, we open ourselves up to hearing

God's voice more clearly, allowing Him to speak to us in ways that we might miss in the midst of noise and activity. Silence in prayer is about being receptive, about listening for God's guidance rather than simply speaking to Him.

Moreover, silence in prayer helps us to develop a deeper awareness of God's sovereignty and majesty. In Psalm 62:5, it says, "My soul, wait thou only upon God; for my expectation is from him." This verse encourages us to wait in silence before the Lord, trusting in His power and His plan for our lives. Silence allows us to step back from our own thoughts and concerns, placing our trust entirely in God and acknowledging that He is in control. In these moments of silent prayer, we are reminded that God is greater than any challenge we face, and that His will is perfect. This deepens our faith and strengthens our relationship with Him, as we learn to rely on His wisdom and timing.

The Bible also connects silence in prayer with the practice of meditation on God's word. In Psalm 1:2, it says, "But his delight is in the law of the Lord; and in his law doth he meditate day and night." Meditation, which involves silent reflection on Scripture, is a key aspect of deepening our prayer life. It allows us to ponder God's word, to let it sink into our hearts, and to apply it to our lives. Silence creates the space for this kind of deep, thoughtful meditation, helping us to internalize God's teachings and to grow in our understanding of His will. By incorporating silence into our prayer life, we make room for God's word to take root in our hearts, transforming us from within.

In addition to meditation, silence in prayer is also associated with waiting on the Lord. In Isaiah 40:31, it says, "But they that wait upon the Lord shall renew their strength; they shall mount up with wings as eagles; they shall run, and not be weary; and they shall walk, and not faint." Waiting on the Lord requires patience and stillness, allowing us to rest in God's presence and to trust in His timing. Silence is an essential part of this waiting, as it helps us to focus on God and to surrender our own desires and anxieties to Him. In the silence of prayer, we learn to be patient, to wait for God's guidance and provision, and to find our strength in Him. This deepens our prayer life by teaching us to trust in God's faithfulness and to rely on His strength rather than our own.

The Bible also teaches that silence in prayer can be a way of expressing our awe and reverence for God. In Habakkuk 2:20, it says, "But the Lord is in his holy temple: let all the earth keep silence before him." This verse calls us to be silent in the presence of God, recognizing His holiness and our own unworthiness. Silence, in this context, is a form of worship, a way of honoring God by acknowledging His greatness and humbling ourselves before Him. In silent prayer, we can reflect on God's majesty, His power, and His love, offering our praise and adoration without the need for words. This deepens our prayer life by cultivating a heart of worship and reverence for the Lord.

Silence in prayer also helps us to cultivate a deeper sense of peace and rest in God's presence. In Matthew 11:28, Jesus invites us, saying, "Come unto me, all ye that labour and are heavy laden, and I will give you rest." While this verse does not explicitly mention silence, the concept of rest is closely tied to the idea of finding peace in God's presence. Silence allows us to enter into that rest, to lay aside our burdens and to find comfort and renewal in the Lord. In the quiet of prayer, we can experience the peace that passes all understanding, the peace that only God can give. This deepens our prayer life by helping us to find true rest in God's presence, where we can be still and know that He is God.

Furthermore, silence in prayer is a way of practicing humility and surrender before God. In James 4:10, it says, "Humble yourselves in the sight of the Lord, and he shall lift you up." Silence helps us to humble ourselves before God, to recognize our dependence on Him, and to surrender our will to His. In silent prayer, we acknowledge that we do not have all the answers, that we need God's guidance and direction in our lives. This humility and surrender deepen our prayer life by bringing us into a closer, more intimate relationship with God, where we can trust Him fully and rely on His wisdom and grace.

The Bible also teaches that silence in prayer can be a way of seeking God's presence in times of trouble and distress. In Psalm 34:17, it says, "The righteous cry, and the Lord heareth, and delivereth them out of all their troubles." While this verse speaks of crying out to God, there are also times when our prayers are silent, when words fail us in the face of overwhelming circumstances. In these moments, silence becomes a form of prayer, a way of seeking God's presence and comfort without the need for words. In the silence, we can pour out our hearts to God, trusting that He hears us and will deliver us from our troubles. This deepens our prayer life by teaching us to rely on God's presence and power, even when we cannot find the words to express our needs.

Silence in prayer is also a way of practicing gratitude and thanksgiving. In 1 Thessalonians 5:18, it says, "In every thing give thanks: for this is the will of God in Christ Jesus concerning you." While this verse encourages us to give thanks in all circumstances, silence can be a powerful way of expressing our gratitude to God. In the quiet of prayer, we can reflect on the many blessings God has given us, offering our thanks and praise without the need for words. Silence allows us to focus on God's goodness and to cultivate a heart of gratitude, deepening our prayer life by helping us to recognize and appreciate God's many gifts.

In addition to gratitude, silence in prayer is also a way of seeking God's guidance and wisdom. In Proverbs 3:5-6, it says, "Trust in the Lord with all thine heart; and lean not unto thine own understanding. In all thy ways acknowledge him, and he shall direct thy paths." Silence helps us to listen for God's direction, to seek His wisdom rather than relying on our own understanding. In silent prayer, we can ask God for guidance, and then wait in stillness for His answer. This deepens our prayer life by teaching us to trust in God's wisdom and to follow His leading in all that we do.

The Bible also connects silence in prayer with the practice of repentance and confession. In Psalm 32:3-5, David reflects on the weight of unconfessed sin, saying, "When I kept silence, my bones waxed old through my roaring all the day long. For day and night thy hand was heavy upon me: my moisture is turned into the drought of summer. Selah. I acknowledged my sin unto thee, and mine iniquity have I not hid. I said, I will confess my transgressions unto the Lord; and thou forgavest the iniquity of my sin. Selah." While David speaks of the burden of silence in hiding sin, this passage also highlights the importance of bringing our sins to God in prayer. Silence in prayer can be a time of self-examination, where we reflect on our actions, acknowledge our sins, and seek God's forgiveness. This deepens our prayer life by bringing us into a place of honesty and repentance before God, where we can experience His mercy and grace.

Furthermore, silence in prayer is a way of waiting for God's justice and deliverance. In Psalm 37:7, it says, "Rest in the Lord, and wait patiently for him: fret not thyself because of him who prospereth in his way, because of the man who bringeth wicked devices to pass." Silence helps us to wait patiently for God's justice, trusting that He will bring about what is right in His own time. In silent prayer, we can bring our concerns and frustrations to God, and then rest in the assurance that He is in control. This deepens our prayer life by teaching us to trust in God's timing and to find peace in His sovereignty.

Silence in prayer is also a way of experiencing God's presence in the midst of life's challenges. In Isaiah 41:10, it says, "Fear thou not; for I am with thee: be not dismayed; for I am thy God: I will strengthen thee; yea, I will help thee; yea, I will uphold thee with the right hand of my righteousness." Silence allows us to focus on God's presence, to remember His promises, and to draw strength from His unwavering support. In the quiet of prayer, we can find comfort and encouragement, knowing that God is with us, no matter what we face.

This deepens our prayer life by helping us to rely on God's presence and power, even in the most difficult times.

In addition to experiencing God's presence, silence in prayer is also a way of seeking His peace. In Philippians 4:6-7, it says, "Be careful for nothing; but in every thing by prayer and supplication with thanksgiving let your requests be made known unto God. And the peace of God, which passeth all understanding, shall keep your hearts and minds through Christ Jesus." Silence in prayer allows us to bring our worries and concerns to God, and then to rest in His peace. It is in the stillness that we can experience the peace that comes from trusting in God's goodness and faithfulness. This deepens our prayer life by helping us to find true peace in God's presence, a peace that transcends all circumstances.

Silence in prayer is also a way of practicing obedience to God. In John 14:15, Jesus says, "If ye love me, keep my commandments." Silence helps us to listen for God's instructions, to be attentive to His word, and to respond in obedience. In silent prayer, we can ask God to reveal His will to us, and then wait in stillness for His guidance. This deepens our prayer life by fostering a spirit of obedience and submission to God's will, helping us to live in a way that is pleasing to Him.

The Bible also teaches that silence in prayer can be a way of seeking God's provision. In Matthew 6:31-33, Jesus encourages us not to worry about our needs, saying, "Therefore take no thought, saying, What shall we eat? or, What shall we drink? or, Wherewithal shall we be clothed? (For after all these things do the Gentiles seek:) for your heavenly Father knoweth that ye have need of all these things. But seek ye first the kingdom of God, and his righteousness; and all these things shall be added unto you." Silence in prayer helps us to focus on seeking God's kingdom first, trusting that He will provide for our needs. In the quiet of prayer, we can bring our requests to God and then rest in the assurance that He will take care of us. This deepens our prayer life by teaching us to rely on God's provision and to prioritize our relationship with Him above all else.

In addition to seeking God's provision, silence in prayer is also a way of waiting for His promises to be fulfilled. In Hebrews 10:23, it says, "Let us hold fast the profession of our faith without wavering; (for he is faithful that promised;)." Silence helps us to hold on to God's promises, to wait patiently for His word to be fulfilled, and to trust in His faithfulness. In silent prayer, we can reflect on God's promises, meditate on His word, and renew our faith in His unchanging character. This deepens our prayer life by helping us to stay grounded in God's promises, even when the fulfillment of those promises seems delayed.

Finally, silence in prayer is a way of cultivating a heart of worship and adoration for God. In Psalm 95:6, it says, "O come, let us worship and bow down: let us kneel before the Lord our maker." Silence helps us to bow down in reverence before God, to offer our worship and praise in a posture of humility and awe. In the quiet of prayer, we can reflect on God's goodness, His greatness, and His love, offering our hearts to Him in worship. This deepens our prayer life by helping us to focus on who God is, rather than just on what He can do for us.

Throughout the Bible, silence is portrayed as a sacred and powerful practice that is essential for deepening our prayer life. By choosing to be silent, we create space to encounter God more intimately, to listen for His voice, and to experience His presence in a profound way. Silence helps us to meditate on God's word, to wait for His guidance, to practice humility and surrender, and to find peace and rest in His presence. It allows us to bring our concerns and needs to God, to seek His provision and promises, and to cultivate a heart of worship and adoration. In a world that is often noisy and distracting, the Bible's teachings on silence offer a different way of living, one that encourages us to be still, to know that God is God, and to deepen our relationship with Him through the sacred art of silence. The Bible, especially in the

King James Version, teaches us that silence is not just the absence of words, but a powerful and intentional practice that can transform our prayer life and draw us closer to God. By embracing the sacred art of silence, we can learn to listen for God's voice, to rest in His presence, and to deepen our faith and love for Him in ways that words alone cannot achieve.

Chapter 8 - Displaying Humility and Reverence

Silence is a profound and sacred concept in the Bible, especially in the King James Version (KJV), where it is closely linked to humility and reverence before God. One of the key verses that highlights the importance of silence in demonstrating humility and reverence is found in Habakkuk 2:20, which says, "But the Lord is in his holy temple: let all the earth keep silence before him." This verse captures the essence of how silence serves as a powerful expression of our recognition of God's majesty and authority. It calls us to be still, to cease from our busyness and distractions, and to approach God with a quiet and humble heart, acknowledging His greatness and our own smallness in comparison. Silence, in this context, is not just the absence of speech; it is an intentional act of reverence, a way of showing deep respect for God's holiness and sovereignty.

The Bible consistently teaches that silence before God is a vital part of our spiritual life, serving as a way to cultivate humility. Humility, as described in Scripture, is the recognition of our dependence on God and our need for His grace. In James 4:10, it says, "Humble yourselves in the sight of the Lord, and he shall lift you up." Silence helps us to humble ourselves before God, to acknowledge that we do not have all the answers, and that we are in need of His wisdom and guidance. In the quietness of our hearts, we can reflect on our own limitations and recognize the greatness of God's power and authority. By choosing to be silent, we make room for God to speak into our lives, to guide us, and to lift us up according to His will.

Silence also plays a crucial role in fostering a sense of reverence for God. Reverence, as the Bible teaches, is the deep respect and awe that we have for God's majesty and holiness. In Psalm 46:10, it says, "Be still, and know that I am God: I will be exalted among the heathen, I will be exalted in the earth." This verse encourages us to be still and silent, to pause and consider who God is, and to acknowledge His exalted position in the universe. Silence allows us to step back from our own thoughts and concerns, to focus entirely on God, and to offer Him the worship and adoration that He deserves. In these moments of silence, we are reminded of God's greatness and our own need to approach Him with humility and reverence.

The Bible also teaches that silence is a way of preparing our hearts to encounter God. In Exodus 3:5, when Moses encounters the burning bush, God says to him, "Draw not nigh hither: put off thy shoes from off thy feet, for the place whereon thou standest is holy ground." This moment is a powerful reminder that when we come into the presence of God, we are entering holy ground, and we must do so with the utmost reverence. Silence helps us to prepare our hearts for these encounters with God, to approach Him with the respect and awe that is due to Him. By being silent, we acknowledge that we are in the presence of the Almighty, and we position ourselves to receive His word and His guidance.

In addition to preparing our hearts, silence also allows us to express our dependence on God. In Psalm 62:5, it says, "My soul, wait thou only upon God; for my expectation is from him." This verse teaches that our hope and trust are in God alone, and that silence is a way of waiting on Him, of demonstrating our reliance on His timing and His provision. When we are silent before God, we are acknowledging that we cannot do everything on our own, that we need His help and His guidance in our lives. Silence becomes a way of surrendering our own will to God's will, of placing our trust in His plans rather than our own. This deepens our relationship with God by fostering a spirit of humility and dependence, recognizing that all we have and all we are comes from Him.

Moreover, silence in the Bible is often associated with the fear of the Lord, which is another way of describing our reverence for God.

In Proverbs 1:7, it says, "The fear of the Lord is the beginning of knowledge: but fools despise wisdom and instruction." The fear of the Lord is not about being afraid of God, but about having a deep respect and awe for His authority and His holiness. Silence helps us to cultivate this fear of the Lord, to approach God with the reverence and respect that He deserves. In the quietness of our hearts, we can reflect on God's majesty, His justice, and His righteousness, and we can respond with the humility and reverence that are appropriate for those who stand in the presence of the Almighty.

The Bible also connects silence with the idea of listening to God. In Ecclesiastes 5:2, it says, "Be not rash with thy mouth, and let not thine heart be hasty to utter any thing before God: for God is in heaven, and thou upon earth: therefore let thy words be few." This verse encourages us to be slow to speak and quick to listen when we are in the presence of God. Silence is a way of showing respect for God's wisdom and authority, of acknowledging that His ways are higher than our ways, and that His thoughts are higher than our thoughts. By being silent, we position ourselves to hear what God has to say, to receive His wisdom and instruction with a humble and receptive heart.

In addition to listening to God, silence also helps us to reflect on our own lives and our relationship with God. In Psalm 4:4, it says, "Stand in awe, and sin not: commune with your own heart upon your bed, and be still." This verse teaches that silence provides an opportunity for self-examination, for reflecting on our actions and our attitudes in light of God's holiness. In the quietness of prayer and meditation, we can consider how we are living our lives, whether we are walking in obedience to God's commands, and whether there are areas where we need to repent jnd seek God's forgiveness. Silence helps us to approach God with a humble and contrite heart, recognizing our need for His mercy and grace.

Furthermore, the Bible teaches that silence is a way of showing respect for others, which is an extension of our reverence for God. In

Proverbs 17:27-28, it says, "He that hath knowledge spareth his words: and a man of understanding is of an excellent spirit. Even a fool, when he holdeth his peace, is counted wise: and he that shutteth his lips is esteemed a man of understanding." These verses suggest that those who are wise and understanding are careful with their words, choosing to speak only when necessary. Silence, in this sense, is a sign of wisdom and humility, showing that we are more interested in understanding others and maintaining peace than in proving ourselves right or winning arguments. By cultivating silence, we demonstrate respect for others and for the image of God in them, recognizing that our words have the power to build up or tear down.

Silence also plays a role in our worship of God, as it allows us to express our awe and wonder at His majesty. In Psalm 95:6, it says, "O come, let us worship and bow down: let us kneel before the Lord our maker." This verse invites us to approach God with a posture of worship, to bow down before Him in reverence and adoration. Silence helps us to enter into this posture of worship, to focus on God's greatness and to offer Him the praise and honor that He is due. In the quietness of worship, we can reflect on God's goodness, His faithfulness, and His love, offering our hearts to Him in humble adoration.

The Bible also teaches that silence is a way of showing respect for God's creation. In Psalm 19:1, it says, "The heavens declare the glory of God; and the firmament sheweth his handywork." This verse reminds us that all of creation testifies to the greatness of God, and that we are called to recognize and respect the beauty and majesty of the world that He has made. Silence allows us to appreciate the wonder of God's creation, to stand in awe of the natural world and to give thanks for the many blessings that God has given us. In the quietness of nature, we can reflect on God's creativity and His care for all that He has made, and we can respond with gratitude and reverence.

In addition to appreciating creation, silence also helps us to cultivate a sense of gratitude for God's provision in our lives. In 1 Thessalonians 5:18, it says, "In every thing give thanks: for this is the will of God in Christ Jesus concerning you." While this verse encourages us to give thanks in all circumstances, silence can be a powerful way of expressing our gratitude to God. In the quietness of prayer, we can reflect on the many blessings that God has given us, offering our thanks and praise without the need for words. Silence allows us to focus on God's goodness and to cultivate a heart of gratitude, deepening our relationship with Him and fostering a spirit of humility and reverence.

Moreover, silence in the Bible is often associated with the idea of waiting on the Lord. In Lamentations 3:26, it says, "It is good that a man should both hope and quietly wait for the salvation of the Lord." This verse teaches that waiting on God requires patience and stillness, allowing us to rest in His presence and to trust in His timing. Silence is an essential part of this waiting, as it helps us to focus on God and to surrender our own desires and anxieties to Him. In the silence of prayer, we learn to be patient, to wait for God's guidance and provision, and to find our strength in Him. This deepens our relationship with God by teaching us to trust in His faithfulness and to rely on His strength rather than our own.

The Bible also teaches that silence is a way of practicing obedience to God. In John 14:15, Jesus says, "If ye love me, keep my commandments." Silence helps us to listen for God's instructions, to be attentive to His word, and to respond in obedience. In silent prayer, we can ask God to reveal His will to us, and then wait in stillness for His guidance. This deepens our relationship with God by fostering a spirit of obedience and submission to His will, helping us to live in a way that is pleasing to Him.

Furthermore, silence in the Bible is often connected with the practice of meditation on God's word. In Psalm 1:2, it says, "But his delight is in the law of the Lord; and in his law doth he meditate day and night." Meditation, which involves silent reflection on Scripture, is a key aspect of deepening our spiritual life. It allows us to ponder God's word, to let it sink into our hearts, and to apply it to our lives. Silence creates the space for this kind of deep, thoughtful meditation, helping us to internalize God's teachings and to grow in our understanding of His will. By incorporating silence into our spiritual practice, we make room for God's word to take root in our hearts, transforming us from within.

In addition to meditation, silence in the Bible is also associated with seeking God's presence in times of trouble and distress. In Psalm 34:17, it says, "The righteous cry, and the Lord heareth, and delivereth them out of all their troubles." While this verse speaks of crying out to God, there are also times when our prayers are silent, when words fail us in the face of overwhelming circumstances. In these moments, silence becomes a form of prayer, a way of seeking God's presence and comfort without the need for words. In the silence, we can pour out our hearts to God, trusting that He hears us and will deliver us from our troubles. This deepens our relationship with God by teaching us to rely on His presence and power, even when we cannot find the words to express our needs.

The Bible also teaches that silence is a way of practicing humility in our relationships with others. In Philippians 2:3, it says, "Let nothing be done through strife or vainglory; but in lowliness of mind let each esteem other better than themselves." This verse encourages us to approach others with humility, to consider their needs and perspectives before our own. Silence helps us to listen more and speak less, to understand others' viewpoints, and to respond with kindness and respect. By cultivating silence in our interactions with others, we demonstrate humility and foster peace and understanding in our relationships.

Moreover, silence in the Bible is often associated with the practice of contentment. In Philippians 4:11, Paul writes, "Not that I speak in respect of want: for I have learned, in whatsoever state I am, therewith to be content." Contentment often involves being silent, accepting our circumstances with grace, and finding peace in the knowledge that God is in control. Silence helps us to practice contentment, to focus on our blessings rather than our wants, and to cultivate a heart of gratitude and peace.

Finally, silence in the Bible is a way of experiencing the peace of God in our hearts. In John 14:27, Jesus says, "Peace I leave with you, my peace I give unto you: not as the world giveth, give I unto you. Let not your heart be troubled, neither let it be afraid." This peace, which surpasses all understanding, is often found in the quiet moments of life, in the times when we set aside the noise and distractions of the world and focus on the presence of God. Silence allows us to enter into this peace, to rest in the assurance of God's love and care, and to find comfort in His presence.

Throughout the Bible, silence is portrayed as a sacred and powerful practice that is essential for cultivating humility and reverence before God. By choosing to be silent, we create space to encounter God more intimately, to listen for His voice, and to experience His presence in a profound way. Silence helps us to meditate on God's word, to wait for His guidance, to practice humility and surrender, and to find peace and rest in His presence. It allows us to bring our concerns and needs to God, to seek His provision and promises, and to cultivate a heart of worship and adoration. In a world that is often noisy and distracting, the Bible's teachings on silence offer a different way of living, one that encourages us to be still, to know that God is God, and to deepen our relationship with Him through the sacred art of silence. The Bible, especially in the King James Version, teaches us that silence is not just the absence of words, but a powerful and intentional practice that can transform our lives and draw us closer to God. By embracing the sacred art of silence, we can learn to listen for God's voice, to rest in His presence, and to deepen our faith and love for Him in ways that words alone cannot achieve. Silence before God is a sign of humility and reverence, acknowledging His majesty and authority, and it is through this sacred practice that we can grow in our relationship with the Almighty and experience the fullness of His grace and love.

Chapter 9 - Disarming Conflict

Silence is a powerful tool in the Bible, particularly in the King James Version (KJV), where it is often associated with wisdom, peace, and the ability to avoid conflict. The sacred art of silence is deeply rooted in Scripture, teaching us how to navigate life's challenges with grace and understanding. One of the most significant verses that illustrate the power of silence in avoiding conflict is Proverbs 15:1, which says, "A soft answer turneth away wrath: but grievous words stir up anger." This verse highlights the importance of how we respond to others, emphasizing that a gentle, quiet response can calm a situation, while harsh, angry words can make it worse. The Bible teaches that silence, or choosing our words carefully, can prevent conflicts from escalating, helping us to maintain peace in our relationships and in our hearts.

The Bible consistently teaches that silence is not just the absence of speech, but a deliberate choice that can lead to better outcomes in difficult situations. When we face conflicts or potential arguments, the natural human reaction might be to respond quickly, often with words that can fuel the fire of disagreement. However, the wisdom found in Scripture reminds us that a soft, calm, and measured response, or even complete silence, can diffuse tension and prevent an argument from becoming more intense. Silence gives us the time to think before we speak, to consider the consequences of our words, and to choose a response that promotes peace rather than strife.

In many instances, silence allows us to step back from a heated situation and avoid saying something we might later regret. The Bible warns us about the dangers of speaking in anger. In Proverbs 29:11, it says, "A fool uttereth all his mind: but a wise man keepeth it in till afterwards." This verse teaches us that it is wise to hold back our immediate reactions, especially when we are upset. By practicing silence, we can control our emotions, avoid saying things in the heat of the moment, and prevent conflicts from escalating. Silence helps us to be thoughtful and intentional with our words, ensuring that what we say is constructive rather than destructive.

Moreover, the Bible also connects silence with patience, which is crucial in avoiding conflict. In Proverbs 14:29, it says, "He that is slow to wrath is of great understanding: but he that is hasty of spirit exalteth folly." This verse emphasizes the value of being slow to anger, which often requires us to be silent and patient, rather than reacting impulsively. Silence gives us the space to calm down, to reflect on the situation, and to respond in a way that promotes understanding and resolution rather than further conflict. By being slow to speak and slow to anger, we create an environment where peace can thrive, and conflicts can be resolved more effectively.

Silence also helps us to listen more and speak less, which is another key aspect of avoiding conflict. In James 1:19, it says, "Wherefore, my beloved brethren, let every man be swift to hear, slow to speak, slow to wrath." This verse teaches us that being quick to listen and slow to speak is a wise approach to communication, especially in potentially contentious situations. By listening more, we can understand the other person's perspective better, which helps to avoid misunderstandings that can lead to conflict. Silence allows us to fully hear what the other person is saying, to process their words, and to respond thoughtfully, rather than reacting impulsively. This approach fosters an atmosphere of mutual respect and understanding, which is essential for resolving disagreements peacefully.

The Bible also shows us that silence can be a way of avoiding unnecessary arguments. In Proverbs 17:14, it says, "The beginning of strife is as when one letteth out water: therefore leave off contention, before it be meddled with." This verse compares the start of a conflict to the letting out of water, which, once begun, is difficult to stop. Silence helps us to "leave off contention," to avoid engaging in arguments that could lead to strife. By choosing to remain silent instead of responding to provocation, we prevent conflicts from starting and maintain peace in our relationships. Silence becomes a way of exercising restraint and wisdom, choosing not to engage in disputes that are likely to escalate.

In addition to preventing conflict, silence also plays a role in de-escalating situations that are already tense. In Proverbs 15:18, it says, "A wrathful man stirreth up strife: but he that is slow to anger appeaseth strife." This verse teaches that anger and hasty speech can stir up conflict, while patience and restraint can calm it. Silence, or a gentle response, helps to diffuse tension and reduce the likelihood of an argument getting out of control. By choosing to be silent or to respond softly, we can help to cool down a heated situation, bringing calm and understanding instead of further agitation. This approach not only helps to avoid conflict but also builds stronger, more peaceful relationships.

Silence is also a way of showing respect for others, which is crucial in maintaining peace and avoiding conflict. In Proverbs 11:12, it says, "He that is void of wisdom despiseth his neighbour: but a man of understanding holdeth his peace." This verse suggests that holding our peace, or remaining silent, can be a sign of understanding and respect for others. Silence shows that we value the other person's perspective and that we are willing to listen and consider their point of view. By being silent, we demonstrate that we are more interested in resolving the issue peacefully than in winning an argument or proving ourselves right. This respect for others is key to avoiding conflict and fostering harmonious relationships.

The Bible also teaches that silence can prevent us from saying things that could hurt others and lead to conflict. In Proverbs 21:23, it says, "Whoso keepeth his mouth and his tongue keepeth his soul from troubles." This verse highlights the protective power of silence, suggesting that by controlling our words, we can avoid unnecessary trouble and conflict. Silence helps us to be mindful of the impact our words can have on others, encouraging us to speak only when necessary and to choose our words carefully. By practicing silence, we can avoid saying things that might escalate a situation or cause harm, thus maintaining peace and harmony in our relationships.

Moreover, silence can help us to avoid the sin of gossip, which is often a source of conflict. In Proverbs 16:28, it says, "A froward man soweth strife: and a whisperer separateth chief friends." Gossip and slander can destroy relationships and create discord among people. By choosing to be silent and refraining from speaking negatively about others, we prevent the spread of harmful words and protect the peace within our communities. Silence, therefore, becomes a tool for preserving harmony and unity, ensuring that our words do not contribute to strife or division.

In addition to preventing gossip, silence also helps us to avoid the sin of anger, which can easily disrupt peace. In Ecclesiastes 7:9, it says, "Be not hasty in thy spirit to be angry: for anger resteth in the bosom of fools." This verse teaches that anger is often the result of hasty, unconsidered reactions. When we speak out of anger, we are more likely to say things that hurt others and cause conflict. Silence, on the other hand, gives us the time to calm down, to think about our response, and to choose words that promote peace rather than anger. By being slow to speak and slow to anger, we create an environment of calm and understanding, where peace can flourish.

Silence is also connected with the idea of humility, which is essential for avoiding conflict. In Philippians 2:3, it says, "Let nothing be done through strife or vainglory; but in lowliness of mind let each esteem other better than themselves." This verse encourages us to approach others with humility, to consider their needs and perspectives before our own. Silence helps us to practice this humility, to listen more and speak less, and to avoid the pride that can lead to conflict. By being silent, we demonstrate that we are willing to put others first, to value their opinions, and to work towards peaceful solutions. This humility is key to avoiding conflict and building strong, healthy relationships.

The Bible also connects silence with the practice of forgiveness, which is crucial for resolving conflicts and maintaining peace. In Colossians 3:13, it says, "Forbearing one another, and forgiving one another, if any man have a quarrel against any: even as Christ forgave you, so also do ye." Forgiveness often requires us to be silent, to refrain from speaking words of anger or resentment, and instead to offer grace and understanding. Silence helps us to let go of grudges, to forgive others, and to restore peace in our relationships. By choosing to be silent rather than voicing our anger, we can promote healing and reconciliation, avoiding the escalation of conflicts.

Furthermore, silence can help us to avoid the sin of judgment, which can lead to conflict. In Matthew 7:1-2, Jesus warns, "Judge not, that ye be not judged. For with what judgment ye judge, ye shall be judged: and with what measure ye mete, it shall be measured to you again." When we are quick to judge others, we often create conflict and division. Silence helps us to refrain from making hasty judgments, to take the time to understand the full situation before we speak. By being slow to judge and quick to listen, we foster an environment of grace and understanding, where peace can thrive.

Silence is also a way of practicing self-control, which is essential for avoiding conflict. In Proverbs 25:28, it says, "He that hath no rule over his own spirit is like a city that is broken down, and without walls." This verse teaches that without self-control, we are vulnerable to all kinds of negative influences, including anger, jealousy, and strife. Silence helps us

to practice self-control, to rule over our own spirit, and to ensure that our words and actions promote peace rather than conflict. By cultivating silence, we cultivate self-control, which in turn fosters peace in our hearts and our relationships.

The Bible also teaches that silence can prevent us from engaging in disputes over trivial matters. In 2 Timothy 2:23-24, it says, "But foolish and unlearned questions avoid, knowing that they do gender strifes.

And the servant of the Lord must not strive; but be gentle unto all men, apt to teach, patient." This verse encourages us to avoid engaging in disputes that are likely to lead to strife. Silence helps us to avoid these unnecessary arguments, to focus on what is truly important, and to promote peace in our interactions with others. By choosing silence over unnecessary debates, we can prevent conflicts and maintain harmony in our relationships.

In addition to avoiding disputes, silence can also be a way of avoiding unnecessary criticism and negative speech, which can disrupt peace. In Ephesians 4:29, it says, "Let no corrupt communication proceed out of your mouth, but that which is good to the use of edifying, that it may minister grace unto the hearers." This verse encourages us to use our words to build others up, rather than to tear them down. Silence helps us to control our speech, to ensure that our words are kind, loving, and edifying. By choosing to be silent rather than speaking negatively, we promote peace and harmony in our relationships.

Moreover, silence can help us to avoid the sin of boasting, which can create tension and conflict. In Proverbs 27:2, it says, "Let another man praise thee, and not thine own mouth; a stranger, and not thine own lips." Boasting, or speaking pridefully about ourselves, can lead to envy, jealousy, and strife. By choosing to be silent instead of boasting, we demonstrate humility and promote peace in our interactions with others. Silence, in this context, is a way of practicing modesty and ensuring that our words do not create unnecessary conflict or competition.

The Bible also teaches that silence can be a way of waiting for God's guidance in difficult situations, which can help us to avoid conflict. In Psalm 37:7, it says, "Rest in the Lord, and wait patiently for him: fret not thyself because of him who prospereth in his way, because of the man who bringeth wicked devices to pass." Silence helps us to wait patiently for God's guidance, to trust that He will show us the right way to handle a situation, and to avoid rushing into conflicts that could be avoided with a little patience. By being silent and waiting on the Lord, we can avoid unnecessary conflicts and find peaceful solutions to our problems.

Finally, silence is a way of experiencing the peace of God in our hearts, which helps us to avoid conflict. In John 14:27, Jesus says, "Peace I leave with you, my peace I give unto you: not as the world giveth, give I unto you. Let not your heart be troubled, neither let it be afraid." This peace, which surpasses all understanding, is often found in the quiet moments of life, in the times when we set aside the noise and distractions of the world and focus on the presence of God. Silence allows us to enter into this peace, to rest in the assurance of God's love and care, and to find comfort in His presence. By cultivating this inner peace through silence, we are better equipped to handle conflicts with grace and understanding, avoiding unnecessary arguments and maintaining harmony in our relationships.

Throughout the Bible, silence is portrayed as a sacred and powerful practice that is essential for avoiding conflict and promoting peace. By choosing to be silent, we create space to listen, to reflect, and to respond thoughtfully, rather than reacting impulsively or angrily. Silence helps us to avoid saying things that could hurt others, to refrain from gossip, and to control our anger. It allows us to practice humility, patience, and self-control, all of which are key to maintaining peaceful relationships. In a world that is often noisy and contentious, the Bible's teachings on silence offer a different way of living, one that encourages us to be mindful of our words and to use our speech to build up rather than to tear down. The sacred art of silence is a timeless and valuable practice that can help us to avoid conflict, to cultivate peace, and to live in harmony with others. The Bible, especially in the King James Version, teaches us that silence is not just the absence of words, but a powerful and intentional practice that can transform our lives and help us to live in peace with God and with others. By embracing the sacred art of silence, we can learn to speak only when necessary, to use our words wisely, and to cultivate a spirit of peace and harmony in all that we do.

Chapter 10 - Deliberating Thoughtfulness

Silence is a powerful and sacred concept in the Bible, especially in the King James Version (KJV), where it is often associated with wisdom, self-control, and the ability to live a thoughtful, intentional life. The Bible teaches us that silence is not just the absence of words but a deliberate choice that encourages us to think carefully before we speak. One of the most significant verses that illustrate the power of silence in promoting thoughtfulness is Proverbs 13:3, which says, "He that keepeth his mouth keepeth his life: but he that openeth wide his lips shall have destruction." This verse highlights the importance of controlling our speech, emphasizing that those who are mindful of their words can protect themselves from harm, while those who speak recklessly can bring about their own downfall. The Bible consistently teaches that silence is a valuable tool that encourages careful thought and reflection, helping us to avoid destructive outcomes and to live a life that is pleasing to God.

In a world where people often speak without thinking, the wisdom of silence stands out as a powerful way to avoid unnecessary trouble and to preserve our well-being. The Bible warns us about the dangers of speaking too quickly or without considering the consequences. When we rush to speak, we are more likely to say things that we may later regret, causing harm to ourselves and others. Silence, on the other hand, gives us the opportunity to pause, to think about what we are going to say, and to choose our words wisely. This thoughtful approach to communication is a hallmark of wisdom and maturity, and it is a key aspect of living a life that honors God.

The Bible often connects silence with self-control, which is essential for encouraging thoughtfulness. In Proverbs 29:11, it says, "A fool uttereth all his mind: but a wise man keepeth it in till afterwards."

This verse teaches us that it is wise to hold back our immediate reactions, especially when we are upset or emotional. By practicing silence, we can control our impulses, take the time to think through our response, and avoid saying things in the heat of the moment that could lead to destructive outcomes. Silence helps us to be patient and deliberate in our communication, ensuring that our words are measured and thoughtful rather than impulsive and harmful.

Moreover, the Bible also connects silence with the practice of listening, which is crucial for encouraging thoughtfulness. In James 1:19, it says, "Wherefore, my beloved brethren, let every man be swift to hear, slow to speak, slow to wrath." This verse teaches us that being quick to listen and slow to speak is a wise approach to communication. By listening more and speaking less, we give ourselves the opportunity to fully understand the situation before we respond. Silence allows us to process what we have heard, to consider our words carefully, and to respond in a way that is thoughtful and appropriate. This approach fosters an atmosphere of understanding and respect, which is essential for maintaining healthy relationships and avoiding unnecessary conflicts.

The Bible also teaches that silence can help us avoid the sin of speaking foolishly or rashly. In Proverbs 17:28, it says, "Even a fool, when he holdeth his peace, is counted wise: and he that shutteth his lips is esteemed a man of understanding." This verse highlights the value of silence in making us appear wise, even if we do not have all the answers. By choosing to remain silent rather than speaking out of turn, we can avoid saying things that might reveal our ignorance or cause harm. Silence, in this context, is a way of demonstrating humility and recognizing that we do not always need to have the last word. It encourages us to think carefully before we speak and to ensure that our words are edifying and beneficial to others.

In addition to avoiding foolish speech, silence also helps us to avoid the sin of gossip, which is often the result of careless or thoughtless words. In Proverbs 16:28, it says, "A froward man soweth strife: and a whisperer separateth chief friends." Gossip and slander can destroy relationships and create discord among people. By choosing to be silent and refraining from speaking negatively about others, we prevent the spread of harmful words and protect the peace within our communities. Silence, therefore, becomes a tool for preserving harmony and unity, ensuring that our words do not contribute to strife or division. This thoughtful approach to communication helps us to maintain strong, healthy relationships and to live in a way that honors God.

Moreover, the Bible teaches that silence can prevent us from saying things that we may later regret. In Proverbs 18:21, it says, "Death and life are in the power of the tongue: and they that love it shall eat the fruit thereof." This verse reminds us of the immense power of our words, which can bring either life or death, blessing or cursing. When we speak without thinking, we risk using our words in a way that brings harm rather than good. Silence, on the other hand, gives us the time to consider the impact of our words, to choose them carefully, and to ensure that they bring life and encouragement rather than destruction. By practicing silence, we can avoid the destructive consequences of careless speech and use our words to build up rather than tear down.

The Bible also connects silence with the idea of guarding our hearts, which is essential for encouraging thoughtfulness. In Proverbs 4:23, it says, "Keep thy heart with all diligence; for out of it are the issues of life." This verse teaches us that our words are a reflection of what is in our hearts, and that we must guard our hearts carefully to ensure that our words are pure and edifying. Silence helps us to take the time to examine our hearts, to consider our motives, and to ensure that our words are a true reflection of the love and grace of God. By being silent, we give ourselves the opportunity to align our hearts with God's will, to think carefully before we speak, and to ensure that our words are a blessing to others.

Moreover, silence encourages us to seek wisdom from God before we speak. In James 1:5, it says, "If any of you lack wisdom, let him ask of God, that giveth to all men liberally, and upbraideth not; and it shall be given him." This verse teaches us that God is the source of all wisdom, and that we should seek His guidance before we speak. Silence gives us the time to pray, to ask God for wisdom, and to wait for His direction before we respond. By seeking God's wisdom in silence, we can ensure that our words are thoughtful, wise, and aligned with His will. This approach helps us to avoid the pitfalls of careless speech and to live a life that is guided by the wisdom of God.

The Bible also teaches that silence can help us to avoid the sin of anger, which can lead to destructive outcomes. In Ecclesiastes 7:9, it says, "Be not hasty in thy spirit to be angry: for anger resteth in the bosom of fools." This verse reminds us that anger is often the result of hasty, unconsidered reactions. When we speak out of anger, we are more likely to say things that hurt others and cause conflict. Silence, on the other hand, gives us the time to calm down, to think about our response, and to choose words that promote peace rather than anger. By being slow to speak and slow to anger, we can avoid the destructive consequences of rash words and maintain peace in our relationships.

Moreover, the Bible connects silence with the practice of humility, which is essential for encouraging thoughtfulness. In Philippians 2:3, it says, "Let nothing be done through strife or vainglory; but in lowliness of mind let each esteem other better than themselves." This verse encourages us to approach others with humility, to consider their needs and perspectives before our own. Silence helps us to practice this humility, to listen more and speak less, and to avoid the pride that can lead to conflict. By being silent, we demonstrate that we are willing to put others first, to value their opinions, and to work towards peaceful solutions. This humility is key to avoiding conflict and building strong, healthy relationships.

The Bible also teaches that silence can prevent us from engaging in disputes over trivial matters. In 2 Timothy 2:23-24, it says, "But foolish and unlearned questions avoid, knowing that they do gender strifes. And the servant of the Lord must not strive; but be gentle unto all men, apt to teach, patient." This verse encourages us to avoid engaging in disputes that are likely to lead to strife. Silence helps us to avoid these unnecessary arguments, to focus on what is truly important, and to promote peace in our interactions with others. By choosing silence over unnecessary debates, we can prevent conflicts and maintain harmony in our relationships.

Moreover, the Bible teaches that silence is a way of practicing self-control, which is essential for encouraging thoughtfulness. In Proverbs 25:28, it says, "He that hath no rule over his own spirit is like a city that is broken down, and without walls." This verse teaches that without self-control, we are vulnerable to all kinds of negative influences, including anger, jealousy, and strife. Silence helps us to practice self-control, to rule over our own spirit, and to ensure that our words and actions promote peace rather than conflict. By cultivating silence, we cultivate self-control, which in turn fosters peace in our hearts and our relationships.

The Bible also connects silence with the practice of waiting on the Lord, which is essential for encouraging thoughtfulness. In Psalm 37:7, it says, "Rest in the Lord, and wait patiently for him: fret not thyself because of him who prospereth in his way, because of the man who bringeth wicked devices to pass." Silence helps us to wait patiently for God's guidance, to trust that He will show us the right way to handle a situation, and to avoid rushing into decisions or actions that could lead to destructive outcomes. By being silent and waiting on the Lord, we can avoid unnecessary conflicts and find peaceful solutions to our problems.

Moreover, the Bible teaches that silence can help us to avoid the sin of boasting, which can lead to destructive outcomes. In Proverbs

27:2, it says, "Let another man praise thee, and not thine own mouth; a stranger, and not thine own lips." Boasting, or speaking pridefully about ourselves, can lead to envy, jealousy, and strife. By choosing to be silent instead of boasting, we demonstrate humility and promote peace in our interactions with others. Silence, in this context, is a way of practicing modesty and ensuring that our words do not create unnecessary conflict or competition.

The Bible also connects silence with the practice of contentment, which is essential for encouraging thoughtfulness. In Philippians 4:11, Paul writes, "Not that I speak in respect of want: for I have learned, in whatsoever state I am, therewith to be content." Contentment often involves being silent, accepting our circumstances with grace, and finding peace in the knowledge that God is in control. Silence helps us to practice contentment, to focus on our blessings rather than our wants, and to cultivate a heart of gratitude and peace.

Finally, the Bible teaches that silence is a way of experiencing the peace of God in our hearts, which helps us to avoid destructive outcomes. In John 14:27, Jesus says, "Peace I leave with you, my peace I give unto you: not as the world giveth, give I unto you. Let not your heart be troubled, neither let it be afraid." This peace, which surpasses all understanding, is often found in the quiet moments of life, in the times when we set aside the noise and distractions of the world and focus on the presence of God. Silence allows us to enter into this peace, to rest in the assurance of God's love and care, and to find comfort in His presence. By cultivating this inner peace through silence, we are better equipped to handle conflicts with grace and understanding, avoiding unnecessary arguments and maintaining harmony in our relationships.

Throughout the Bible, silence is portrayed as a sacred and powerful practice that is essential for encouraging thoughtfulness and promoting a life that is pleasing to God. By choosing to be silent, we create space to listen, to reflect, and to respond thoughtfully, rather than reacting impulsively or angrily. Silence helps us to avoid saying things that could hurt others, to refrain from gossip, and to control our anger. It allows us to practice humility, patience, and self-control, all of which are key to maintaining peaceful relationships. In a world that is often noisy and contentious, the Bible's teachings on silence offer a different way of living, one that encourages us to be mindful of our words and to use our speech to build up rather than to tear down. The sacred art of silence is a timeless and valuable practice that can help us to avoid destructive outcomes, to cultivate peace, and to live in harmony with others. The Bible, especially in the King James Version, teaches us that silence is not just the absence of words, but a powerful and intentional practice that can transform our lives and help us to live in peace with God and with others. By embracing the sacred art of silence, we can learn to speak only when necessary, to use our words wisely, and to cultivate a spirit of peace and harmony in all that we do.

Chapter 11 - Driving Spiritual Growth

Silence is a deeply meaningful concept in the Bible, particularly in the King James Version (KJV), where it is closely connected with spiritual growth, strength, and reliance on God. The Bible teaches that silence is not merely the absence of noise or speech but a powerful spiritual practice that fosters a deeper relationship with God, enabling us to grow in faith, strength, and wisdom. One of the most profound verses that highlight the significance of silence in promoting spiritual growth is found in Isaiah 30:15, which says, "For thus saith the Lord God, the Holy One of Israel; In returning and rest shall ye be saved; in quietness and in confidence shall be your strength: and ye would not." This verse emphasizes that our spiritual strength and salvation are not found in frantic activity or self-reliance but in returning to God, resting in His presence, and embracing the quiet confidence that comes from trusting in Him. Silence, in this context, is a vital component of spiritual growth, providing the space and stillness needed to connect with God on a deeper level and to develop a quiet confidence in His power and provision.

The Bible consistently teaches that spiritual growth is a process that requires us to step back from the busyness of life, to be still, and to listen for God's voice. In a world filled with noise and distractions, silence becomes a sanctuary where we can retreat and refocus our hearts and minds on God. It is in these moments of quiet reflection that we are able to hear God's gentle whispers, to receive His guidance, and to grow in our understanding of His will for our lives. Silence helps us to cultivate a heart that is sensitive to the leading of the Holy Spirit, enabling us to grow spiritually as we learn to discern God's voice amidst the clamor of the world.

Moreover, the Bible connects silence with the idea of resting in God's presence, which is essential for spiritual growth. In Psalm 46:10, it says, "Be still, and know that I am God: I will be exalted among the heathen, I will be exalted in the earth." This verse calls us to be still, to cease from our striving and to rest in the knowledge that God is in control. Silence allows us to enter into this rest, to quiet our hearts and minds, and to focus entirely on God. In these moments of stillness, we are reminded that our strength comes not from our own efforts but from our reliance on God. This quiet confidence in God's sovereignty and care is a key aspect of spiritual growth, as it teaches us to trust in Him more fully and to depend on His strength rather than our own.

Silence also plays a crucial role in helping us to return to God, as Isaiah 30:15 suggests. The verse speaks of "returning" as a pathway to salvation, indicating that spiritual growth often involves turning away from our own ways and returning to God with a repentant and humble heart. Silence provides the space for this return, allowing us to reflect on our lives, to recognize where we have strayed, and to seek God's forgiveness and guidance. In the quietness of prayer and meditation, we can examine our hearts, confess our sins, and recommit ourselves to following God's ways. This process of returning to God is an essential part of spiritual growth, as it renews our relationship with Him and strengthens our commitment to living according to His will.

Furthermore, the Bible teaches that silence is linked with the development of inner strength, which is vital for spiritual growth. In Proverbs 18:14, it says, "The spirit of a man will sustain his infirmity; but a wounded spirit who can bear?" This verse highlights the importance of a strong and healthy spirit in sustaining us through life's challenges. Silence, by fostering a deep connection with God, helps to strengthen our spirit, enabling us to endure trials and difficulties with confidence and grace. In the stillness, we can draw strength from God's presence, allowing His peace and power to fill our hearts and sustain us through whatever challenges we face. This inner strength, rooted in our quiet confidence in God, is a hallmark of spiritual maturity and growth.

Moreover, the Bible connects silence with the practice of waiting on the Lord, which is essential for spiritual growth. In Lamentations 3:25-26, it says, "The Lord is good unto them that wait for him, to the soul that seeketh him. It is good that a man should both hope and quietly wait for the salvation of the Lord." Waiting on the Lord requires patience, trust, and a willingness to be silent and still before Him. Silence helps us to cultivate this patience and trust, teaching us to wait for God's timing and to rely on His wisdom rather than our own understanding. In these moments of quiet waiting, we grow in our faith as we learn to trust in God's plan and to depend on His provision. This waiting in silence is a key aspect of spiritual growth, as it deepens our relationship with God and strengthens our confidence in His faithfulness.

The Bible also teaches that silence is a way of practicing humility, which is essential for spiritual growth. In Micah 6:8, it says, "He hath shewed thee, O man, what is good; and what doth the Lord require of thee, but to do justly, and to love mercy, and to walk humbly with thy God?" Walking humbly with God requires us to recognize our dependence on Him and to approach Him with a quiet and reverent heart. Silence helps us to cultivate this humility, as it encourages us to listen more and speak less, to seek God's wisdom rather than relying on our own, and to acknowledge our need for His guidance and grace. By embracing silence, we can grow in humility, recognizing that our spiritual strength comes not from our own efforts but from our reliance on God.

Moreover, the Bible connects silence with the practice of meditation on God's word, which is crucial for spiritual growth. In Psalm 1:2, it says, "But his delight is in the law of the Lord; and in his law doth he meditate day and night." Meditation involves silent reflection on Scripture, allowing God's word to sink deeply into our hearts and minds. Silence creates the space for this kind of deep, thoughtful meditation, helping us to internalize God's teachings and to apply them to our lives. By meditating on God's word in silence, we can grow in our understanding of His will and in our ability to live according to His commands. This practice of silent meditation is a key aspect of spiritual growth, as it helps us to align our thoughts and actions with the truth of God's word.

Furthermore, the Bible teaches that silence is a way of seeking God's presence in times of trouble and distress, which is essential for spiritual growth. In Psalm 34:17, it says, "The righteous cry, and the Lord heareth, and delivereth them out of all their troubles." While this verse speaks of crying out to God, there are also times when our prayers are silent, when words fail us in the face of overwhelming circumstances. In these moments, silence becomes a form of prayer, a way of seeking God's presence and comfort without the need for words. In the silence, we can pour out our hearts to God, trusting that He hears us and will deliver us from our troubles. This deepens our spiritual growth by teaching us to rely on God's presence and power, even when we cannot find the words to express our needs.

The Bible also connects silence with the idea of resting in God's peace, which is vital for spiritual growth. In Philippians 4:6-7, it says, "Be careful for nothing; but in every thing by prayer and supplication with thanksgiving let your requests be made known unto God. And the peace of God, which passeth all understanding, shall keep your hearts and minds through Christ Jesus." Silence in prayer allows us to bring our worries and concerns to God and then to rest in His peace. It is in the stillness that we can experience the peace that comes from trusting in God's goodness and faithfulness. This deepens our spiritual growth by helping us to find true peace in God's presence, a peace that transcends all circumstances and strengthens our hearts and minds.

Moreover, the Bible teaches that silence is a way of practicing obedience to God, which is essential for spiritual growth. In John 14:15, Jesus says, "If ye love me, keep my commandments." Silence helps us to listen for God's instructions, to be attentive to His word, and to respond in obedience. In silent prayer, we can ask God to reveal His will to us, and then wait in stillness for His guidance. This deepens our spiritual growth by fostering a spirit of obedience and submission to God's will, helping us to live in a way that is pleasing to Him.

Furthermore, the Bible teaches that silence is a way of practicing contentment, which is crucial for spiritual growth. In Philippians 4:11, Paul writes, "Not that I speak in respect of want: for I have learned, in whatsoever state I am, therewith to be content." Contentment often involves being silent, accepting our circumstances with grace, and finding peace in the knowledge that God is in control. Silence helps us to practice contentment, to focus on our blessings rather than our wants, and to cultivate a heart of gratitude and peace.

The Bible also teaches that silence is a way of experiencing the peace of God in our hearts, which is essential for spiritual growth. In John 14:27, Jesus says, "Peace I leave with you, my peace I give unto you: not as the world giveth, give I unto you. Let not your heart be troubled, neither let it be afraid." This peace, which surpasses all understanding, is often found in the quiet moments of life, in the times when we set aside the noise and distractions of the world and focus on the presence of God. Silence allows us to enter into this peace, to rest in the assurance of God's love and

care, and to find comfort in His presence. By cultivating this inner peace through silence, we are better equipped to handle conflicts with grace and understanding, avoiding unnecessary arguments and maintaining harmony in our relationships.

Throughout the Bible, silence is portrayed as a sacred and powerful practice that is essential for encouraging thoughtfulness and promoting a life that is pleasing to God. By choosing to be silent, we create space to listen, to reflect, and to respond thoughtfully, rather than reacting impulsively or angrily. Silence helps us to avoid saying things that could hurt others, to refrain from gossip, and to control our anger. It allows us to practice humility, patience, and self-control, all of which are key to maintaining peaceful relationships. In a world that is often noisy and contentious, the Bible's teachings on silence offer a different way of living, one that encourages us to be mindful of our words and to use our speech to build up rather than to tear down. The sacred art of silence is a timeless and valuable practice that can help us to avoid destructive outcomes, to cultivate peace, and to live in harmony with others. The Bible, especially in the King James Version, teaches us that silence is not just the absence of words, but a powerful and intentional practice that can transform our lives and help us to live in peace with God and with others. By embracing the sacred art of silence, we can learn to speak only when necessary, to use our words wisely, and to cultivate a spirit of peace and harmony in all that we do.

Chapter 12 - Demonstrating Trust in God

Silence is a powerful and sacred concept in the Bible, particularly in the King James Version (KJV), where it is closely linked with demonstrating trust in God. The Bible teaches us that silence is not just the absence of words, but a deliberate and meaningful act that can reflect our faith and reliance on God's provision and protection. One of the most profound verses that illustrates the significance of silence in demonstrating trust in God is found in Exodus 14:14, which says, "The Lord shall fight for you, and ye shall hold your peace." This verse emphasizes the idea that we do not always need to defend ourselves or respond to every challenge with words, because God is our defender. By choosing to remain silent in the face of adversity, we show that we trust God to handle the situation, believing that He will fight our battles for us and that His strength is far greater than anything we can muster on our own.

The Bible consistently teaches that trust in God is a fundamental aspect of our faith, and silence is often portrayed as an expression of that trust. In moments of fear, uncertainty, or conflict, our natural instinct may be to speak out, to defend ourselves, or to try to control the situation with our words. However, the Bible encourages us to take a different approach, one that involves quieting our hearts and trusting in God's sovereign power. Silence, in this sense, becomes a way of surrendering our own need to control the outcome and placing the situation entirely in God's hands. It is an acknowledgment that God is in control, that He sees what we cannot see, and that His ways are higher than our ways. By holding our peace, we are essentially saying, "Lord, I trust You to fight this battle for me. I know that You are with me, and I believe that You will protect me and provide for me."

Moreover, the Bible connects silence with the idea of waiting on God, which is closely related to trust. In Psalm 27:14, it says, "Wait on the Lord: be of good courage, and he shall strengthen thine heart: wait, I say, on the Lord." Waiting on the Lord requires patience and faith, and silence is an important part of this waiting process. It allows us to be still and to focus on God's presence, to listen for His guidance, and to trust in His timing. Silence helps us to resist the urge to take matters into our own hands or to speak prematurely. Instead, it encourages us to wait for God to act, knowing that His timing is perfect and that He will strengthen our hearts as we trust in Him. This kind of trust is not passive; it is an active, intentional choice to rely on God's wisdom and to believe that He is working on our behalf, even when we cannot see it.

The Bible also teaches that silence can be a powerful response in the face of accusations or opposition, demonstrating our trust in God to vindicate us. In Isaiah 53:7, it says, "He was oppressed, and he was afflicted, yet he opened not his mouth: he is brought as a lamb to the slaughter, and as a sheep before her shearers is dumb, so he openeth not his mouth." This verse speaks of Jesus, who chose to remain silent during His trial, even though He was unjustly accused and condemned. Jesus' silence was not a sign of weakness, but of profound trust in God's plan and purpose. He knew that God would ultimately vindicate Him, and He did not feel the need to defend Himself with words. In the same way, we can choose silence as a way of trusting that God will defend us and that we do not always need to respond to every criticism or accusation. By holding our peace, we demonstrate that we believe in God's justice and that we trust Him to take care of us.

Furthermore, the Bible connects silence with peace, which is often a result of trusting in God. In Psalm 46:10, it says, "Be still, and know that I am God: I will be exalted among the heathen, I will be exalted in the earth." This verse encourages us to be still, to quiet our hearts and minds, and to recognize God's sovereignty. Silence allows us to enter into that stillness, to rest in the knowledge that God is in control and that we do not need to be anxious or fearful. By choosing to be silent, we create space for God's peace to fill our hearts, and we demonstrate our trust in His ability to handle whatever challenges we may be facing. This peace is a direct result of our trust in God, and it is a powerful testimony to those around us of the strength and stability that comes from relying on Him.

The Bible also teaches that silence can be a way of avoiding unnecessary conflict and trusting God to bring about resolution. In Proverbs 15:1, it says, "A soft answer turneth away wrath: but grievous words stir up anger." This verse highlights the power of a gentle, quiet response in diffusing tension and preventing conflict from escalating. By choosing to be silent or to respond softly, we demonstrate our trust that God can bring about peace and resolution, even in difficult situations. We do not need to rely on our own words or arguments to defend ourselves; instead, we can trust that God will work in the hearts of those involved and that He will bring about the best outcome. Silence, in this context, is an act of faith, showing that we believe in God's power to transform and heal relationships.

Moreover, the Bible connects silence with humility, which is closely related to trust in God. In James 4:10, it says, "Humble yourselves in the sight of the Lord, and he shall lift you up." Humility involves recognizing our own limitations and acknowledging our dependence on God. Silence helps us to practice this humility, as it encourages us to listen more and speak less, to seek God's wisdom rather than relying on our own, and to trust that He will lift us up in His time. By choosing silence, we demonstrate that we are willing to submit to God's will and to trust Him to work in our lives. This humility is a key aspect of trusting in God, as it shows that we believe that His ways are better than our ways and that His plans are higher than our plans.

The Bible also teaches that silence can be a way of practicing patience, which is an important aspect of trust. In Lamentations 3:26, it says, "It is good that a man should both hope and quietly wait for the salvation of the Lord." Waiting on the Lord requires patience, and silence is a crucial part of this waiting process. It allows us to be still, to focus on God's presence, and to trust in His timing. Silence helps us to resist the urge to act impulsively or to speak out of turn. Instead, it encourages us to wait for God to act, knowing that His timing is perfect and that He will bring about the best outcome. This kind of patience is a sign of deep trust in God, showing that we believe in His wisdom and that we are willing to wait for His salvation.

Moreover, the Bible teaches that silence can be a way of experiencing God's presence and finding strength in Him. In Isaiah 30:15, it says, "For thus saith the Lord God, the Holy One of Israel; In returning and rest shall ye be saved; in quietness and in confidence shall be your strength: and ye would not." This verse emphasizes the importance of returning to God, resting in His presence, and finding strength in quiet confidence. Silence allows us to return to God, to rest in Him, and to draw strength from His presence. By being silent, we demonstrate our trust in God's ability to save us and to provide for us. This quiet confidence is a key aspect of trusting in God, as it shows that we believe in His power and that we are willing to rely on Him rather than on our own efforts.

The Bible also connects silence with the practice of contentment, which is closely related to trust in God. In Philippians 4:11, Paul writes, "Not that I speak in respect of want: for I have learned, in whatsoever state I am, therewith to be content." Contentment involves trusting that God will provide for our needs and that He is in control of our circumstances. Silence helps us to practice contentment, as it allows us to focus on our blessings rather than our wants, and to rest in the knowledge that God is taking care of us. By choosing silence, we demonstrate our trust in God's provision and our contentment with what He has given us. This contentment is a sign of deep trust in God, showing that we believe that He knows what is best for us and that He will provide for us in His time.

Moreover, the Bible teaches that silence can be a way of experiencing God's peace, which is a direct result of trusting in Him. In John 14:27, Jesus says, "Peace I leave with you, my peace I give unto you: not as the world giveth, give I unto you. Let not your heart be troubled, neither let it be afraid." This peace, which surpasses all understanding, is often found in the quiet moments of life, in the times when we set aside the noise and distractions of the world and focus on the presence of God. Silence allows us to enter into this peace, to rest in the assurance of God's love and care, and to find comfort in His presence. By cultivating this inner peace through silence, we demonstrate our trust in God and our belief that He is in control. This peace is a powerful testimony to those around us, showing that we trust in God's ability to take care of us and that we are not afraid of what the future holds.

Throughout the Bible, silence is portrayed as a sacred and powerful practice that is essential for demonstrating trust in God. By choosing to be silent, we

create space to listen, to reflect, and to respond thoughtfully, rather than reacting impulsively or defensively. Silence helps us to avoid saying things that could hurt others, to refrain from gossip, and to control our anger. It allows us to practice humility, patience, and self-control, all of which are key to maintaining peaceful relationships and trusting in God's plan. In a world that is often noisy and contentious, the Bible's teachings on silence offer a different way of living, one that encourages us to be mindful of our words and to use our speech to build up rather than to tear down. The sacred art of silence is a timeless and valuable practice that can help us to avoid destructive outcomes, to cultivate peace, and to live in harmony with others. The Bible, especially in the King James Version, teaches us that silence is not just the absence of words, but a powerful and intentional practice that can transform our lives and help us to live in peace with God and with others. By embracing the sacred art of silence, we can learn to speak only when necessary, to use our words wisely, and to cultivate a spirit of peace and harmony in all that we do. Silence, as taught in Scripture, is a profound expression of trust in God, showing that we believe in His power to fight our battles, to provide for our needs, and to guide us in all things. When we hold our peace and trust in God, we demonstrate our faith in His sovereignty and our reliance on His strength, knowing that He will take care of us in every situation.

Conclusion

As you turn the final pages of "The Sacred Art of Silence - How Silence Speaks in Scripture," it is my hope that you have discovered the profound beauty and transformative power of silence as revealed in the Bible. In a world that thrives on noise, where constant communication is often mistaken for connection, you have journeyed through Scripture to uncover a different truth: that in silence, we find clarity, wisdom, and the voice of God. The teachings of the Bible invite us to embrace silence not as an absence, but as a presence—a sacred space where we encounter God, grow in faith, and cultivate peace within our hearts.

Throughout this book, we have explored how silence is woven into the fabric of biblical narratives, from the quiet moments of reflection in the lives of the prophets to the stillness that accompanied Jesus in His most profound moments of prayer. We have seen how silence can guard our souls, deepen our prayer lives, and help us navigate the challenges of life with grace and wisdom. Silence, as Scripture reveals, is not a passive act but an active engagement with the divine, a way of listening more intently, of trusting more deeply, and of aligning ourselves with God's will.

Now, as we reach the conclusion of this journey, the question arises: how do we proceed? How do we carry the lessons of silence into our daily lives in a world that rarely pauses for breath? The answer lies in intentional practice, in making space for silence amidst the busyness of life. It is about creating moments where you can withdraw from the noise, turn inward, and connect with God. Whether it's through dedicated times of silent prayer, moments of reflection during your day, or simply choosing to listen more and speak less, embracing silence is a deliberate choice that can transform your spiritual life.

Start by setting aside time each day for silence. This doesn't need to be lengthy; even a few minutes of quiet can make a profound difference. Use this time to meditate on Scripture, to listen for God's voice, or simply to rest in His presence. As you practice silence, you may find that it brings a deeper sense of peace, clarity, and strength. You may also find that it enhances your ability to listen—to others, to yourself, and to God.

Moreover, let the lessons of silence influence how you interact with the world around you. In conversations, practice listening with an open heart, resisting the urge to fill every gap with words. In moments of conflict, consider the power of a gentle, quiet response. And in times of uncertainty, remember the wisdom of holding your peace, trusting that God is at work even when you cannot see it.

As you move forward, let silence become a sacred rhythm in your life, a counterbalance to the noise and busyness that so often dominate our days. Let it be a reminder that in the quiet, God speaks most clearly. The sacred art of silence is not just a practice; it is a way of being that draws us closer to the heart of God, that strengthens our faith, and that equips us to navigate the complexities of life with grace and wisdom.

In the end, silence is not something to be feared or avoided, but something to be embraced and cherished. It is in the silence that we find God, that we find ourselves, and that we discover the deep, abiding peace that only He can give. As you leave these pages behind, may you carry the sacred art of silence with you, letting it guide you, inspire you, and transform your walk with God.

Don't miss out!

Visit the website below and you can sign up to receive emails whenever Joshua Rhoades publishes a new book. There's no charge and no obligation.

https://books2read.com/r/B-A-AJLBB-VFKUE

BOOKS 2 READ

Connecting independent readers to independent writers.

Did you love *The Sacred Art of Silence - How Silence Speaks in Scripture*? Then you should read *Flee Fornication: The Plea For Purity*[1] by Joshua Rhoades!

[2]

"Flee Fornication - The Plea For Purity" is an essential read for anyone grappling with the challenges of maintaining sexual purity in a world that often glorifies the opposite. This book dives deep into the spiritual and moral pitfalls that can ensnare individuals, drawing them away from a life of purity and toward a path of destruction. It doesn't shy away from addressing the real temptations and struggles that believers face daily, offering a candid look at the consequences of fornication, both spiritually and physically. Grounded in Scripture, calls readers to heed the biblical plea found in 1 Corinthians 6:18, where the Apostle Paul urges, "Flee fornication. Every sin that a man doeth is without

---

1. https://books2read.com/u/3GLqln

2. https://books2read.com/u/3GLqln

the body; but he that committeth fornication sinneth against his own body." This verse serves as the cornerstone of the book, emphasizing the severe spiritual implications of sexual immorality. From the story of Joseph fleeing Potiphar's wife to David's tragic fall with Bathsheba, the book illustrates the importance of vigilance and the devastating consequences of yielding to temptation. It also highlights the power of God's grace and the importance of repentance and restoration for those who have stumbled. The book doesn't just focus on the negative aspects but also provides uplifting encouragement on how to live a life of purity, including practical steps such as setting boundaries, avoiding compromising situations, and seeking accountability. The author stresses that purity is not just about saying "no" to sin but about saying "yes" to a deeper relationship with God. By committing to purity, believers can experience a closer walk with God, free from the guilt and shame that sexual sin brings. The book also considers the role of the Holy Spirit in empowering believers to overcome temptation and live a life that honors God. It is a call to action for those who desire to live a life that reflects the holiness of God, reminding readers that their bodies are temples of the Holy Spirit, and they are called to honor God with their bodies (1 Corinthians 6:19-20). "Flee Fornication - The Plea For Purity" is a powerful and timely message for a generation bombarded with sexual temptation, offering hope, healing, and a path to victory through Christ.